BATTLES, BOATS & BONES

Archaeological Discoveries in Northern Ireland 1987 - 2008

Edited by Emily Murray & Paul Logue

A CIP catalogue record for this book is available from the British Library.
A Library of Congress CIP catalogue record has been applied for.

First published 2010

ISBN 978-0-337-09592-4

Printed in Northern Ireland by W & G Baird

This book is dedicated to our friend and colleague David Wilkinson (1946–2008). He is greatly missed.

Plate i David Wilkinson (NIEA).

Contents

Plate ii Excavation of the tidal mill at Nendrum (NIEA).

List of plates

Front cover

Back cover

Chapter cover images

List of figures

Foreword

This book may be seen as the logical follow-on from *Pieces of the Past*, by Drs Hamlin and Lynn, 1988 and might alternatively have been entitled *Pieces of the Past II*. However, it has a fresh new title instead to reflect the fresh new information within.

This volume contains new information about both the everyday and special aspects of the lives of our predecessors in Northern Ireland. The discoveries written about in the pages that follow are extraordinary and thought provoking. For example, most of us think of Portrush as a modern day seaside resort; however, archaeological excavations there have shown that sometime between 3,000 and 4,000 years ago, during the Bronze Age, it was the site of a village of more than 70 houses. This prehistoric village is of great importance for our knowledge of the past and is unparalleled elsewhere in Ireland.

At Edenderry, the Giant's Ring has long been known of and has been visited by many generations of people. However, recent excavation there has revealed that the above-ground henge monument is just one part of a much wider prehistoric ceremonial landscape, most of which is now only preserved below ground, as archaeological remains. Using the evidence from nearby excavations we can now envisage that the view northwards, from the banks of the Giant's Ring, towards Black Mountain, would once have been dominated by a large timber temple, parts of which may well have been similar in appearance to Stonehenge.

Excavation has also revealed aspects of the craft and technological skills possessed by some of our ancestors. The elegant Bronze Age gold ornaments found near Killymoon demonstrate their great skill in metalwork as does the magnificent Medieval Drumadoon bell shrine.

Plate iii The Drumadoon bell shrine (NIEA).

We are reminded, through the figure of the crucified Christ that came from Limoges in southern France but which formed part of the Drumadoon shrine, that we inhabit an island where long-distance trade, involving seafaring and boatbuilding, has been an important part of our heritage. The Neolithic logboat discovered on the seabed at Greyabbey Bay presents further evidence of this heritage in the form of a seagoing craft that is some 5,000 years old.

The discoveries presented here illustrate both how diverse and exciting our archaeological heritage is, and, that historic monuments come in a wide variety of forms. It is fascinating to contemplate how such unprepossessing lands as school playing fields, eroding bogs, ex-army compounds, waste ground and disused factories can conceal the important relics and everyday remnants of our ancestors.

The Built Heritage Directorate of the Northern Ireland Environment Agency is, in part, tasked with, and committed to, making such information accessible to the wider community. Through publication of this book we have taken another significant step forward towards achieving that goal and I would like to offer my congratulations to all those involved in that. I also wish all of you, its readers, enjoyment in browsing through, or in studying, its pages.

Michael D.A. Coulter
Director: Built Heritage

Preface

The aim of this book is to publicise the results of a selection of archaeological investigations carried out in Northern Ireland over the last two decades and also to acknowledge the huge changes that have taken place in archaeology during this period. In the 1970s and '80s, archaeology was a very different profession to the one it is today, practised on a relatively small scale predominantly by employees of the government and members of staff of the universities. In the late 1990s, changes made to planning policies introduced improved measures for the protection of cultural heritage including archaeological mitigation in advance of development. This policy change, accompanied by a boom in the economy, has led to a massive upsurge in the number of archaeological excavations undertaken annually (Figure i) and an unprecedented level of private sector development-led and developer-funded archaeological activity.

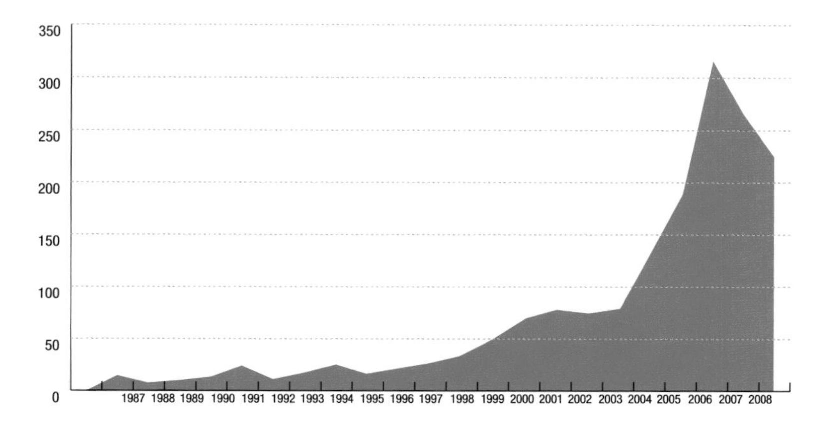

Figure i Graph showing the number of archaeological excavation licences issued by the NIEA from 1987 to 2008 (data for 2005–2008 supplied by the NIEA; earlier data sourced from the Excavations Bulletin).

All archaeological sites require particular consideration in the context of development. Under the new guidelines, planning approval may be conditional on specific archaeological work being carried out, or on changes being made to the layout or design of a development to reduce the impact on the archaeology. The archaeological investigation of a site proposed for development is a multi-stage process starting with a desk-based study of the area under consideration. This background research identifies features and areas of recorded and probable archaeological activity, as many archaeological sites display no surface visibility.

The fieldwork, in many cases, comprises monitoring of mechanical topsoil stripping by an archaeologist followed up by the excavation of any archaeological features uncovered. The work undertaken can vary enormously in scale from a one-person, one-day job of monitoring the excavation of a pit for a septic tank to an extensive project relating to a housing development or new road scheme covering many acres. The archaeological results from the latter large-scale sites have been incredibly significant, with much new valuable information being discovered allowing archaeologists to provide a better narrative and context for the lives of our ancestors in Northern Ireland.

It is a requirement by law that all archaeological excavations in Northern Ireland are carried out under licence issued by the Department of the Environment (DoE) of Northern Ireland. The particular branch of the DoE that issues these licences is termed the Historic Monuments Unit,

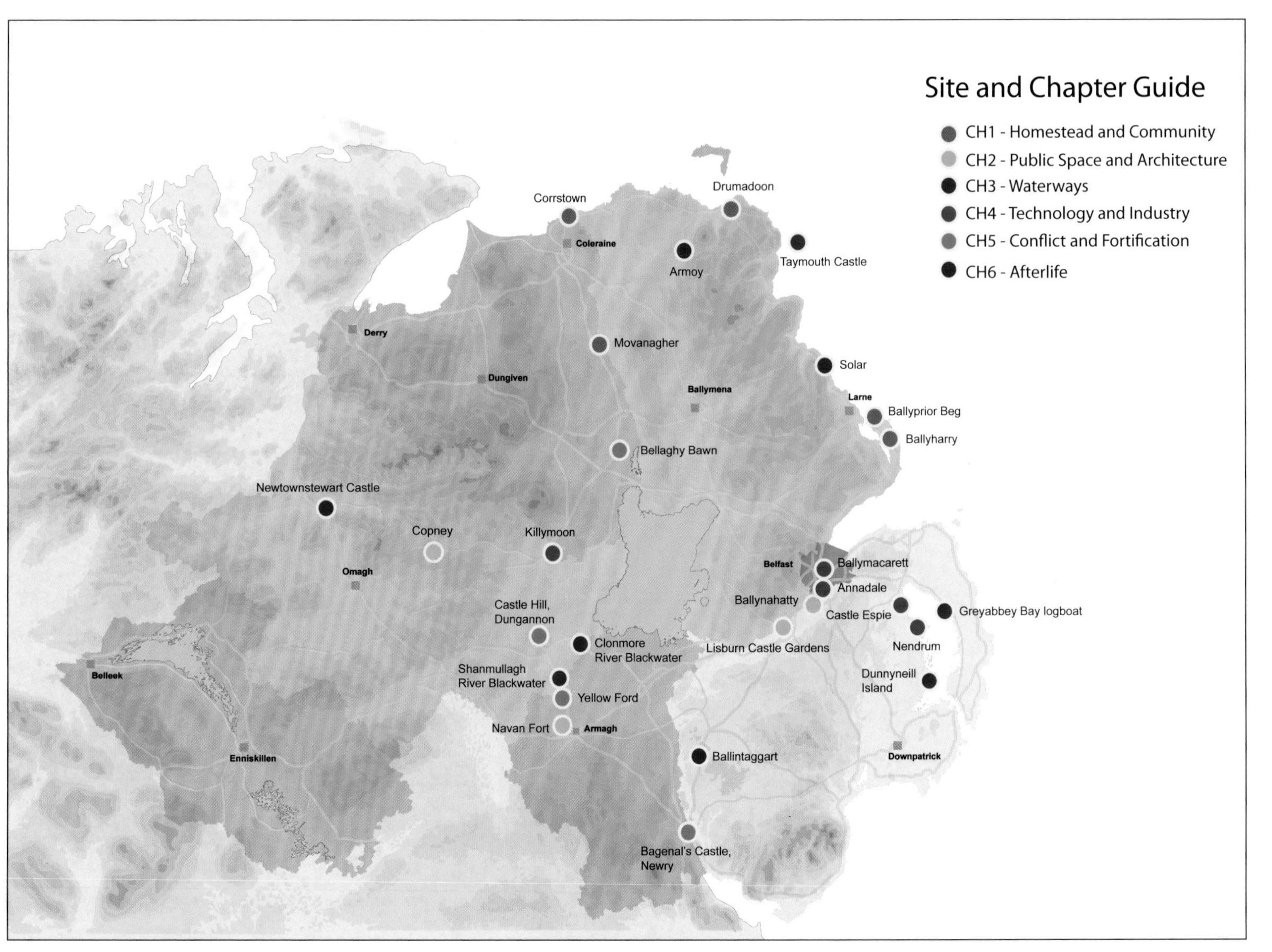

Figure iii Map showing distribution of sites featured in this book.

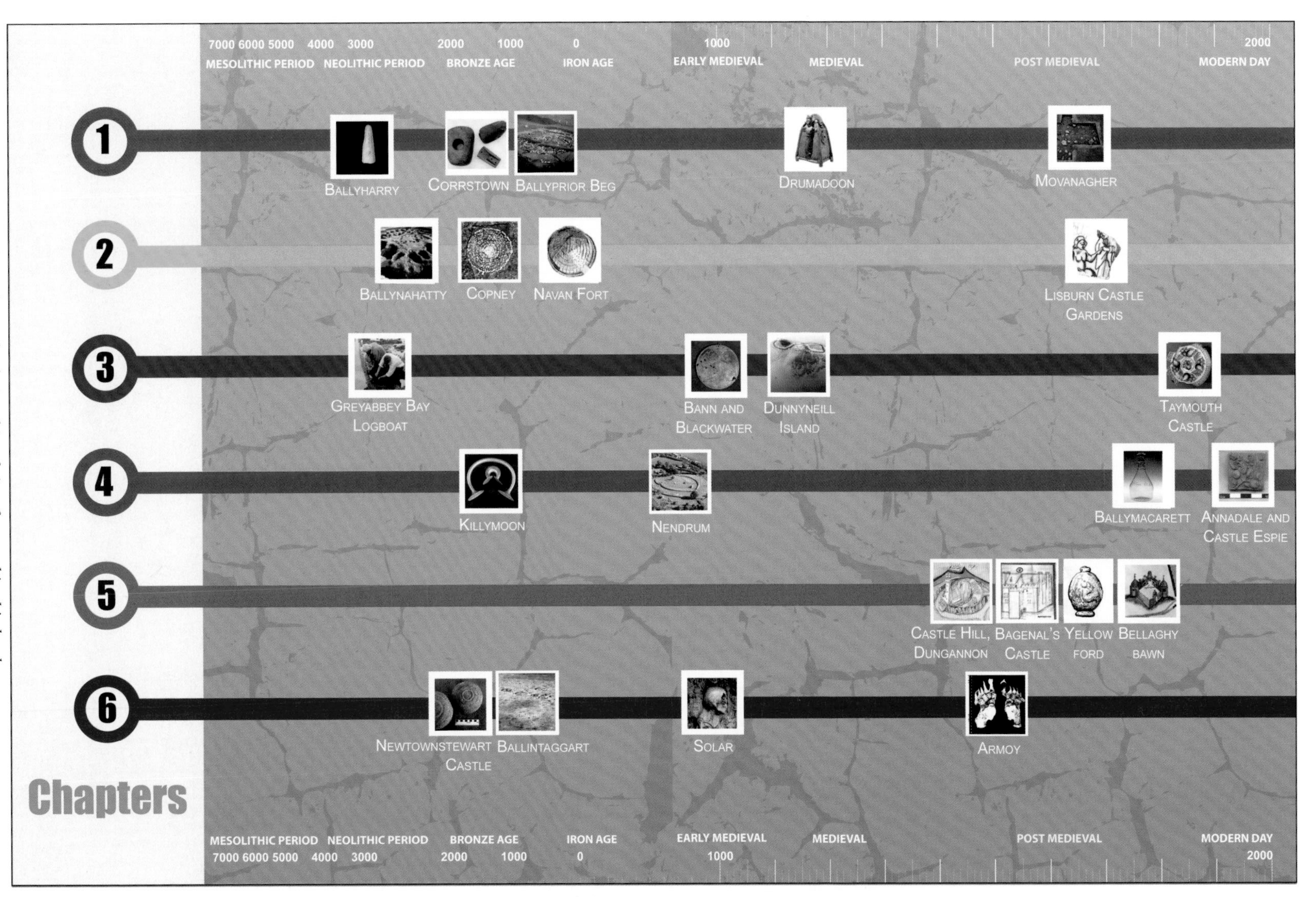

Figure iv Timeline showing chronological relationship of sites featured in this book.

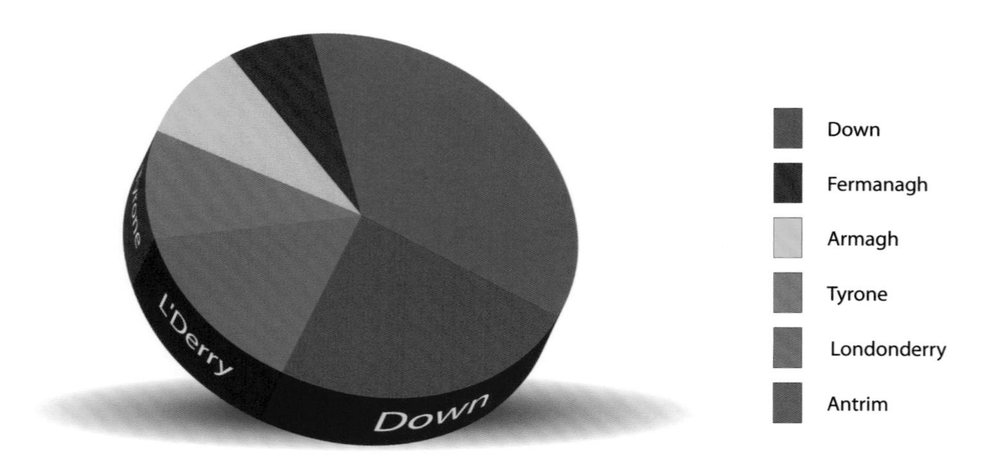

Figure ii Distribution of licences issued by county, from 1987 to 2008 inclusive (source of data as per Figure i).

which is a part of the Built Heritage Directorate of the Northern Ireland Environment Agency (NIEA). One of the terms of this licence is that a full detailed and illustrated report of the excavation is lodged with the Department on completion of the excavation which then becomes part of the Northern Ireland Monuments and Buildings Record (MBR) and can be consulted by the public. Although the majority of archaeological excavations undertaken in any given year are necessitated and financed by the development sector, many excavations are also undertaken with financial support from the NIEA. On behalf of the Northern Ireland public the NIEA also conducts archaeological excavations and surveys of sites under threat from erosion or general deterioration, or as part of the processes of conservation and restoration of historic sites and monuments in its care. The excavations selected for inclusion in this book reflect many aspects of Northern Ireland's heritage. They include sites dating from early prehistory up to the nineteenth century, rural and urban sites, and publicly and privately funded projects. The greater number of developments in the east of the province has meant that there is a geographical bias in the sites selected (Figures ii and iii).

As a thematic approach has been adopted, sites were also chosen based on their relevance to the selected topics – *Homestead and community; Public space and architecture; Waterways; Technology and industry; Conflict and fortification;* and *Afterlife*. The idea of bringing the sites together under these broad headings is to allow comparisons to be drawn on what are common concerns in all periods. The contributors were asked to focus on particular aspects of a site reflecting these themes, and consequently their reports do not necessarily give a full account of all features encountered on the excavations. Further information on the sites can be found in site-specific publications, and details of these follow the relevant articles.

Within each chapter the featured sites are arranged chronologically. Both the Chronological Background that follows this Preface, and chapter introductions, provide some context for the sites that follow and where there is overlap between themes and sites, cross-reference is made to articles that appear elsewhere in the book. The Appendices include a list of the abbreviations used and explanations of keywords along with suggested further reading and useful websites. Site-specific information (years of excavation, institutions and companies involved etc.) is listed in the table at the very end of the book. General acknowledgments are also included in the Appendices. Many of the excavations discussed in this book date from the period before 2008 when the NIEA was known as Environment and Heritage Service (EHS). However, for the sake of consistency, NIEA will be used throughout the publication.

Chronological Background

The timeframe under discussion in this volume covers a period of some 7,000 years, the largest portion of which falls within the prehistoric era. The following overview lists the main site types, artefacts and events associated with the different chronological phases, prehistoric and historic, with a bias towards those aspects that are relevant to sites that are featured within this volume. Further explanation for some of the terms used can be found in Keywords (Appendix 2).

The oldest sites discussed in this book date to the Early Neolithic period. The start of the **Neolithic** (around 4000–2500 BC) is marked by the migration of the first farmers to Ireland bringing with them domestic animals and plants, and new technologies. This new way of life and culture, a radical change from the hunter-gatherer lifestyle that went before, transformed the landscape, as forests were cleared for pasture and to grow crops. Semi-permanent buildings were constructed for a more settled lifestyle (Plate iv) and megalithic ('large stone') tombs such as portal tombs, court tombs and passage tombs, and other ritual monuments were erected. In particular towards the end of the Neolithic, large circular henges were constructed. Stone circles and wedge tombs were also built at the very end of the Neolithic and into the Early Bronze Age. The earliest production of pottery in Ireland can be dated to the Early Neolithic while industrial activity from this time centred on the exploitation of stone resources, in particular flint and porcellanite both of which were primarily sourced in County Antrim. The Neolithic stone toolkit included flint knives, scrapers and arrowheads, and polished stone axes.

Plate iv Two Neolithic rectangular houses at Ballintaggart defined by linear slot-trenches and internal post-holes (NIEA).

The **Bronze Age** (around 2500–500 BC) marks the introduction of metalworking to Ireland and the use of copper, bronze (copper and tin alloy) and gold. The period can be subdivided into the Early (2500–1500 BC), Middle (1500–1200 BC) and Late (1200–500 BC) Bronze Age though these divisions are primarily based on the development of metalworking skills and technologies, and the different styles and complexities of the objects produced. As well as metalwork, much of the evidence for this period comes from burials which display huge variability (see Chapter 6). Bronze Age houses are typically circular in plan while the vast majority of burnt mounds, '*fulachta fiadh*', the commonest prehistoric site type recorded in Ireland, date to the Bronze Age. Over the centuries Bronze Age society became increasingly wealthy, stratified and warlike, with the development of an aristocratic warrior elite by the Late Bronze Age. This hierarchical culture reached its peak between the eighth and sixth centuries BC, and is represented by a wealth of weaponry, tools and gold ornaments, much of which has been recovered in hoards and as votive deposits from watery locations. Other archaeological remains from the Late Bronze Age include hilltop settlements, hillforts and crannogs, and with burials represented almost exclusively by cremations.

The transition from the Bronze Age to the **Iron Age** (around 500 BC–AD 400) appears to have coincided with a deterioration in the climate and increasing wetness, indicated by a rapid growth in peat and the construction of extensive trackways across wetlands. This is a 'Dark Age' in Irish archaeology with a dearth of finds and sites. Those that are recorded include ceremonial centres such as Navan Fort, the continued use of some hillforts and a series of linear earthworks which are presumed to be related to land divisions and territoriality. Evidence for settlement largely consists of hearths and pits and other scattered remains that have returned Iron Age radiocarbon dates. Of iron itself, there is only a small number of surviving Iron Age artefacts. This can, in part, be explained by the fact that iron corrodes easily, but surviving artefacts also suggest that bronze was the principal metal of the period. The spread of iron technology across Europe is associated with a distinct culture that includes chariot burials, fortified hilltop sites, and a curvilinear art-style known as La Tène. It is also assumed that a form of Irish, a Celtic language, was spoken at the time of its adoption in Ireland but it is not known if this language was introduced with iron technology or earlier, in the Late Bronze Age. The nature of this pre-literate, pagan, Celtic-speaking society is a complex topic and heavily embellished in later writings, such as the *Táin Bó Cúailnge* (The Cattle Raid of Cooley) and other tales in the Ulster Cycle.

The Celtic era in Western Europe was brought to an end by the rise of the **Roman Empire**. Ireland was never part of this empire but the proximity of Roman Britain meant that there was inevitably contact between the two islands during the first to fifth centuries AD, and Roman objects, including coins and burials, have been found here.

The **Early Medieval** period (also known as the Early Christian period, AD 400–1177) is marked by the introduction of Christianity, traditionally by the arrival of St Patrick in AD 432. The Church brought a new organisational structure to Ireland but most importantly, introduced literacy. The earliest script used in Ireland is ogham (fourth to sixth centuries AD) which is primarily confined to stone carvings. The surviving documentary sources from this time are written in Latin and Old Irish, and include annals, Saints' Lives, poetry and Old Irish law texts (seventh to ninth centuries AD). The main archaeological field monument of this period is the rath or ringfort. These were enclosed farmsteads of the landholding classes and are the most numerous archaeological monument found in Ireland. Other contemporary site-types are houses, souterrains, crannogs and watermills. It is largely an aceramic period apart from some imported vessels such as E-Ware (possibly containers of wine or oils), and the indigenous Souterrain Ware which is largely confined to the north-east of Ireland.

The lasting impact of the Romans in Western Europe is the introduction of Christianity, with monasticism spreading across Ireland in the sixth century. Monasteries became centres of population (religious and lay), learning, trade and craft production and there has been much discussion as to whether these functioned as 'proto towns'. Most early ecclesiastical buildings were built in organic materials and do not survive while many early ecclesiastical sites have continued in use or have been heavily reconstructed making it difficult to investigate early Church archaeology. Features that do survive include enclosures around early Church sites, cemeteries of inhumation burials (typically orientated east-west), carved stone crosses and pillars, shrines, small stone churches and round towers. The last of these present the first real stone architecture and use of mortar in Ireland. Much fine secular and religious metalwork was produced during this period, as well as illuminated manuscripts, and many of the techniques and designs employed are similar to those of Anglo-Saxon England.

The Age of the **Vikings** across northern Europe dates to the ninth and tenth centuries AD, and the Vikings who attacked and settled in Ireland were mainly Norse. Documentation for their history and exploits is principally from the annals, along with place-name evidence. The Vikings established a number of trading ports, most notably Dublin, and they had settlements also in Carlingford and Strangford in the north of Ireland. Archaeologically the remains of these settlements provide the best physical evidence for their presence in Ireland while a number of Viking burials and hoards (Plate v), typically dominated by silver, have also been recorded.

Plate v Ornaments and ingots of gold, silver and bronze, including a gold finger-ring in Hiberno-Viking style, from Shanmullagh, County Armagh (reproduced courtesy of the Trustees of National Museums Northern Ireland).

Early Medieval Ireland was a hierarchical society, politically divided into over 100 small kingdoms. Over the tenth, eleventh and twelfth centuries these petty kingdoms amalgamated giving rise to a series of influential dynasties and provincial kings. There were five provinces (Ulster, Leinster, Munster, Connacht and Meath) with Meath being the seat of the High King of Ireland. In 1168 the deposed King of Leinster solicited help from King Henry II and successfully returned from England with Anglo-Norman and Cambro-Norman troops. The King of Leinster regained his title but the foreign mercenaries proceeded to make their own territorial claims and took control of parts of Ireland. The latter included John de Courcy who, in 1177, converted about a quarter of Ulster (most of the eastern counties of Antrim and Down) into the Earldom of Ulster. This 'invasion' marks the end of the Early Medieval period and start of the **Anglo-Norman** period, in Ireland (late twelfth to mid fourteenth century). The earls built stone castles, most notably Carrickfergus Castle, while the castles of the barons were of earth and timber ('mottes'). A number of self-governing towns were also established at Carrickfergus, Coleraine, Downpatrick, Newtownards and Antrim. As with secular power, religious power also became increasingly concentrated around this time and in the mid twelfth century the Irish Church was reformed with the establishment of an independent territorial diocesan and parochial structure to bring it into line with much of the rest of Europe. Bishoprics and archbishoprics were established throughout Ireland and new monastic orders, such as the Cistercians and Augustinians, were introduced.

There are major changes across Ireland in the fourteenth century marking the transition to the **Late Medieval** period (1350–1550). Less than two centuries after the Anglo-Norman invasion, the authority of the English Crown in Ireland was much reduced and was in effect restricted to a relatively small area around Dublin ('the Pale'). Political power outside of the Pale was shared by Anglo-Irish (Gaelicised Anglo-Normans and Cambro-Normans) and Gaelic lordships. The principal defensive structures of the Gaelic and Anglo-Irish lords during the fifteenth and sixteenth centuries were tower-houses, while a number of crannogs were also refurbished at this time.

The Reformation and Plantations in Ireland are traditionally seen as marking the transition to the **Post-Medieval** period (around 1550–1800). In the late 1530s the English crown, under Henry VIII, took renewed interest in Ireland. In part this was stimulated by the English Reformation with the dissolution of the monasteries in Ireland transpiring in the 1540s. When his daughter Elizabeth I ascended the throne in 1558, English interest in Irish affairs intensified. There were early attempts to plant English colonists in parts of Leinster and Munster, which led to a series of uprisings while attempts made by the Crown to quell the power of the Irish lords in Ulster led to open warfare and the Nine Years' War (1593–1603). The Gaelic and Gaelicised lords formed an alliance under Hugh O'Neill, Earl of Tyrone and despite a string of Irish victories against the Crown, the rebels under O'Neill were decisively defeated in 1601 at the Battle of Kinsale. The rebels' lands were confiscated and planted with loyal subjects of the Crown. The Plantation of Ulster was the organised colonisation of the province by people from Britain and was the biggest and most successful of the plantation schemes in Ireland. Private plantation by wealthy landowners

Plate vi The surviving round flanking tower at Bellaghy Bawn (NIEA).

began earlier in the sixteenth century mainly in Counties Antrim and Down, while official plantation controlled by the monarchy under the auspices of King James I, was initiated in 1609 in the present day counties Donegal, Londonderry, Tyrone, Fermanagh, Cavan and Armagh. The colonists were mostly from Scotland and England, Presbyterian and Anglican respectively, and the settlements were planned with streets and market places. The new settlements also included the residences of the planters which took the form of tower-houses and manor houses enclosed by a bawn (Plate vi). One of the legacies of the Plantation is the detailed surveys and maps that were made of the colonised territory.

In terms of the economy, Ireland remained largely agricultural until the end of the eighteenth century when it changed to having an industrial base. In the late seventeenth century there was an improvement in communications, growth in the ironworks industry and in the production of fine pottery and linen textiles for export. This economic growth and prosperity is reflected in the fine architecture of the eighteenth century, represented by both private and public buildings such as Florence Court in County Fermanagh and Antrim Court House and by specialised structures, in particular those built for industry (saw mills, flour mills, bleach works, breweries), engineering works (canals, aqueducts, windmills) and the military. Unlike earlier periods, much of Post-Plantation, Post-Medieval archaeology is represented by upstanding buildings as well as by below-ground archaeology.

The Comon
8—1—0
Wheat Hill
26—1—0
Bay of Bang
Bangor
Myln
The Hill hill by the Mill Lead.
The Ball Greene
The Borehill

CHAPTER 1

Homestead and Community

Chapter 1: Homestead and Community

Introduction

This chapter focuses on the house, the domestic and private realm of the family, and on communities where we find evidence for one or more dwellings in proximity. The 'homestead' is represented by the physical remains of a building, though more often than not, all that survives archaeologically is the trace of a house plan accompanied by a range of artefacts.

In Ireland throughout prehistory and into the Medieval period, houses were built predominantly of organic materials. Being susceptible to rot and decay from the damp climate these houses were not long lived and had to be repaired and replaced. The archaeological evidence for these structures therefore survives as below-ground features. These are features dug into the earth such as post-holes and stake-holes that would have housed earthfast, upright timbers and stakes, and linear slot-trenches that would have held a series of closely-set vertical planks or posts, often supported by packing-stones. Occasionally the charred or waterlogged remains of these posts survive in their original place, as at Ballyharry (see later in this chapter). The exact method of walling is rarely possible to reconstruct as, apart from a few exceptional circumstances, the materials used to fill in the gaps and render the walls leave no archaeological trace. Evidence for roofing techniques and materials is even less frequently recovered though the presence, or absence, of internal post-holes and spacing of wall posts can allow some speculation as to the design of the roof.

In some instances, traces also survive of the activities carried out in and around a residence such as food preparation or craftworking. Where preservation conditions are favourable, the recovery of animal bones and charred plant remains can provide information on diet and reflect domestic cleanliness (or lack of), and also afford insights into the world beyond the home and the use of the wider landscape. It is the presence of these sorts of materials, the detritus from day-to-day living and in particular a hearth, found in association with small domestic-scale structures that identify the traces of certain buildings as 'houses'. The evidence, however, can often be ambiguous due to incomplete preservation or excavation. This invites speculation on the interpretation of the features and the possibility that although domestic in scale some structures identified as houses may have had other uses.

The archaeological evidence for houses in Ireland becomes more evident in the Early Neolithic period when solid structures representative of increasingly sedentary farming communities were first built. Rectangular house design predominated across Ireland and indeed across much of Western Europe at this time (see Plate iv and the section on Ballyharry below) and radiocarbon dates for these structures suggest that they were widely and rapidly adopted from around 3700 BC. A shift towards circularity in house design is, however, evident as the Neolithic progresses. This trend continues into the Bronze Age where the vast majority of domestic structures so far excavated are circular in plan (see for example Ballyprior Beg and Corrstown later in this chapter). Evidence for Iron Age domestic settlements in Ireland is elusive and the limited structural evidence that survives is dominated by ritual complexes, although again circular structures predominate (see Navan Fort, Chapter 2). In the Early Medieval period evidence for structural remains is often fragmentary, as at Drumadoon (see later in this chapter), but stratigraphic and scientific dating evidence has demonstrated that there was a trend to change from circular-plan buildings at the beginning of the period (up to around AD 800) to rectilinear structures towards the end. It is clear that circularity in design prevails for domestic structures throughout the prehistoric period and into the first millennium AD in Ireland with the notable exception being the rectangular structures of the Early Neolithic.

Settlements dating to the English earldom in Ulster are typified by stone castles, mottes and the development of early urban settlements such as Carrickfergus. In contrast, contemporary native Gaelic settlement from this time, both within the earldom and further west, is largely invisible. Re-occupation of raths is recorded from the period, as at Drumadoon for example (see later in this chapter), but without documentation it is not possible to determine the ethnicity of those occupants. In the fifteenth and sixteenth centuries the archaeological record for domestic structures is again dominated by the gentry as represented by stone-built tower-houses. Although these have defensive features, they primarily served as dwellings with living quarters, including fireplaces, windows and latrines, typically found in the upper storeys (see Dungannon and Newry, both in Chapter 5). In the seventeenth century there are pictorial maps identifying the approximate locations of a variety of houses, yet even with these maps they are still often difficult to find. For example, only ephemeral traces of the native thatched houses and timber-framed English houses were discovered during excavations at the plantation settlement of Movanagher (see later in this chapter).

The evidence available on early house building in Ireland has hugely increased over the last couple of decades. This is due to the accelerated rate of archaeological discovery following changes in planning policies, and extensive redevelopments. One of the most significant aspects of these substantial area excavations is that they have demonstrated that, more often than not, houses were not isolated. At both Ballyharry and Ballyprior Beg one complete house and part of a second were uncovered while at Corrstown, topsoil stripping of a large area unveiled a dense organised settlement of over 70 structures. At Corrstown also, unenclosed Early Medieval buildings set outside of the rath were recorded. These large-scale excavations have therefore provided context for houses and allow us to at least speculate on the dynamics and scale of earlier communities.

Antiquarian excavations, and excavations carried out in the 1960s, '70s and '80s, largely concentrated on recorded or upstanding monuments. In terms of domestic settlement these were typically biased towards those built in stone or enclosed by earthworks. In contrast, recent infrastructural and housing developments generally avoid upstanding monuments and instead provide an arguably unbiased view of the below-ground archaeological record. It is intriguing therefore that Early Neolithic rectangular houses and circular Bronze Age houses have been found with repeated regularity, while gaps in the domestic settlement record, most notably from the Iron Age and for the native population (those who did not live in castles) during the Anglo-Norman period and succeeding centuries continue to persist. The increased number and better quality of radiocarbon dates that have been produced over recent decades have also suggested that widespread phenomena such as Early Neolithic rectangular houses and Early Medieval raths were adopted quite rapidly across the country. This improved, and improving, dating allows us to question and investigate other aspects of society, such as the economy and environment, to determine the causation for these building phenomena.

Houses provide one of the best insights into the economic and social structure of earlier societies. The holistic approach to the cycle of life and death of these early communities is also suggested by the votive or ritual foundation and closing deposits discovered at many sites including Ballyharry and Ballyprior Beg. These aspects of households coupled with the often only ephemeral remains of the actual structures themselves indicate that, although huge leaps have been made in our understanding, much is yet to be discovered and understood about the basic aspects of the day-to-day lives of our predecessors.

Early Neolithic farmers at Ballyharry on Islandmagee, County Antrim

Dermot Moore and Norman Crothers

Set on a long ridge some 110m above sea level on Islandmagee and overlooking Larne Lough is the townland of Ballyharry. In 1996, during the construction of a gas pipeline from Ballylumford on Islandmagee southwards to Carrickfergus, two Early Neolithic rectangular-plan houses were uncovered at Ballyharry during topsoil stripping of the pipeline corridor.

The two house sites, separated by a distance of 300m, were first observed as dense areas of charcoal-rich, black soil containing prehistoric pottery sherds, flint and other stone tools. Only House 1 was completely excavated, while House 2 was partially investigated. The limited excavation of House 2 revealed that it was a sturdy rectangular-plan structure of post and plank construction and the few finds recovered comprised Neolithic pottery, both shouldered ('carinated') and unshouldered ('uncarinated') bowls, flint implements and polished stone axe fragments. As House 2 was left substantially unexcavated, only House 1 will be discussed in detail here.

One of the unique aspects of House 1 was the complex sequence of occupation involving periods of construction, destruction, reconstruction and eventual abandonment which radiocarbon dating indicates spanned a period between 4032 and 3635 BC. At the time of writing, no other Early Neolithic houses have yet been discovered in Ireland displaying such a sequence of activity and wealth of artefacts.

The earliest phase of activity comprised a sub-rectangular, post-built structure, 13m by 6.5m with its long axis aligned north-north-west/south-south-east and parallel to the gently sloping contours of the ridge (Figure 1.1). Defining its outline were large stone-packed post-holes cut into the basalt bedrock. These would each have held a large wooden post, while three internal double post-holes divided the building into two compartments. The double post-holes would also have been necessary architectural features to support a pitched roof. Occupation of this house may have been short-lived as there was evidence that the wooden posts were removed from the post-holes possibly for use in the next phase of construction.

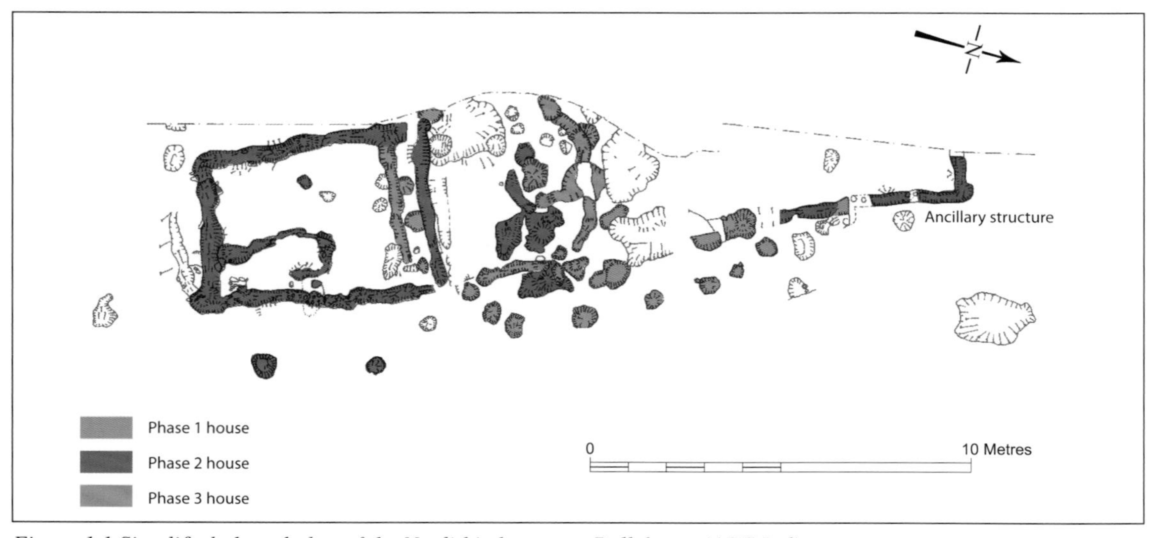

Figure 1.1 Simplified phased plan of the Neolithic houses at Ballyharry (ADS Ltd).

A small quantity of pottery comprising round-bottomed, carinated and uncarinated bowls was recovered from this, and all subsequent phases, of the site. A range of flint knapping debris, the flint being derived from nodules in the local chalk, and flint implements such as scrapers, knives and two arrowheads were also recovered. The only item of personal ornamentation found was a portion of a highly polished greenstone bead. The presence of polished and unpolished flakes of porcellanite, mined at Tievebulliagh in the Antrim Plateau, provides evidence that stone axes were being worked and reworked on site. One artefact of particular note was a stone ard point (Plate 1.1), an early form of ploughshare. This implement, although broken, provides clear evidence of agriculture in the form of land tillage. The identification of the charred remains of wheat grains along with the presence of saddle querns and rubbing stones illustrates that processing of cereals into meal and flour was also part of the domestic activities on site. In addition, the recovery of a small range of wild fruit seeds and nuts such as hazel nuts indicates that the foraging of wild resources was carried out.

Plate 1.1 A stone ard point found in a large post-pit belonging to the first phase of activity of the house at Ballyharry (ADS Ltd).

Partially overlying this first structure and laid out on the same alignment, was a sub-rectangular single-roomed house built of posts and planks and measuring 6.8m by 5m with an entrance in the north-east corner (Figure 1.1). Unlike the earlier house, the foundations comprised stone-packed linear trenches. These trenches were also cut into the bedrock and contained the charred remains of the posts and planks used in the house's construction. The roof of the structure had been supported by two internal posts set along the central east-west axis of the house while two relatively shallow post-pits were uncovered along the exterior eastern side and these too may have been structural. Another internal feature was a possible bedding area defined by a thin slot-trench set in the south-eastern corner.

The remains of a rectangular ancillary structure, possibly of wattle and daub or wicker construction and defined by a poorly preserved L-shaped slot, were uncovered to the north of the main house (Figure 1.1). The area between these two structures contained several shallow pits rich in artefacts.

Artefacts from this second phase of occupation comprised a larger quantity but a similar range of Neolithic pottery sherds as found with the earlier house. A similar range of flint knapping debris and flint implements, such as scrapers and simple retouched pieces, was also recovered with an increase in the number of flint knives and arrowheads. Implements associated with the grinding of grain continued in use, with analysis of the charred cereal remains showing that barley was also being grown in addition to wheat. The presence of barley indicates that these early farmers at Ballyharry were expanding their crop husbandry repertoire. The recovery of quantities of burnt animal bone also illustrates that a mixed farming economy was taking place.

It is in the next phase of activity that the image of peaceful farming communities normally attributed to the Neolithic inhabitants of Ireland is dispelled. This breakdown of community life is clearly shown by the destruction of portions of the main house by an intense fire. The best evidence for burning was found in the northern gable with the remains of burnt posts and planks and heat-fractured packing stones, still in their original places.

The destruction of the rectangular structure appears to have been deliberate, possibly arising out of conflict with a neighbouring farming community. The presence of 34 leaf-shaped and laurel-leaf flint arrowheads, several of which were represented only by their burnt tips and butts, provides good evidence for a violent attack. The burnt arrowhead portions would seem to indicate that they were shot as fire arrows primarily into the northern gable to set the structure alight.

Sometime after this episode of conflict, a period of rebuilding and renovation was undertaken. This saw the reconstruction of the four walls and the addition of an apsidal annex onto the rebuilt north gable giving the house a new overall length of 12m (Figure 1.1). At the same time an east-west partition slot was constructed which ran parallel to the northern wall. The apsidal annex comprised bedding trenches with small amounts of stone packing, suggesting that the annex was of a flimsy construction. Within the confines of the annex, a sub-circular hearth-pit was discovered filled with a series of distinct deposits indicating that a number of fires had been lit in it.

It was within this phase of rebuilding that evidence of an intriguing aspect of ritual activity was uncovered. From the fills of two post-holes in the western and eastern walls of the house were recovered a basalt stone axe and a perfect laurel-leaf arrowhead, deposited blade edge and point downwards respectively. Perhaps these artefacts should be seen as votive offerings defining the end of a period of conflict and the beginning of a period of peaceful reconstruction.

This house appears to have continued in use for a considerable period before its final abandonment. The abandonment of the house is clearly shown by the removal of a corner post (probably to be reused elsewhere) and capping of the subsequent void by a large basalt stone and by the removal of some of the remaining posts and planks from the other wall slots. There is also evidence that this last act of desertion may have seen the burning of the remains of the house.

From this excavated evidence at Ballyharry we now have a more vivid image of life in the Early Neolithic. The picture illustrates that these early farmers were not only self-sufficient in food and raw materials but that they survived a period of conflict by rebuilding and expanding. The site's abandonment signifies the end of the settlement at Ballyharry and the beginning of a new era of nomadic Neolithic pastoralists with their reliance on cattle, new pottery forms, and more ephemeral house sites.

Further reading

Crothers, N. 1996 'Ballyharry's game', *Archaeology Ireland* 10(4), 12–14.

Moore, D.G. 2004 'Hostilities in Early Neolithic Ireland: trouble with the new neighbours. The evidence from Ballyharry, County Antrim'. In, A. Gibson and A. Sheridan (eds), *From sickles to circles*, 142–154. Stroud: Tempus.

The Ballyprior Beg settlement, Islandmagee, County Antrim

Ian Suddaby

Tucked away inland from the sandy beach at Brown's Bay on Islandmagee near Larne in County Antrim lies the Bronze Age settlement in Ballyprior Beg. Built about 3,200 years ago, it was inhabited for perhaps 100 years. The settlement was well sheltered, being situated on a valley floor. The inhabitants lived in environmentally friendly, heat- and fuel-efficient roundhouses, too big and sophisticated to be called huts. They were farmers who kept animals and grew crops and they had few traded goods.

Our evidence for this ancient past comes from archaeological excavations, conducted in 2000 during the work to lay an electrical cable from Scotland to Ireland, across Islandmagee. One complete circular house and a portion of a second were excavated representing just a small part of the settlement. The cable route was only 20m wide, thus setting the parameters of the excavation. The fields, tracks, drains and other assorted farming remains that may have been associated with a settlement like Ballyprior Beg were not found. Their existence must be assumed, using evidence from other sites, aerial photography or analogies with modern agricultural practices in a similar environment.

All of the construction materials needed for the Bronze Age settlement were gathered from the surrounding area; wood from felled trees, raw clay from under the topsoil and stones gathered from the fields. Straw, a by-product of the cereals grown for food, may have been used to thatch

Plate 1.2 Photo of the excavated house (House 1) at Ballyprior Beg: the circular paved interior of the house is in the centre, with fragments of the outer wall in the foreground and the circle of the clay mass-wall-base between them (CFA Archaeology Ltd).

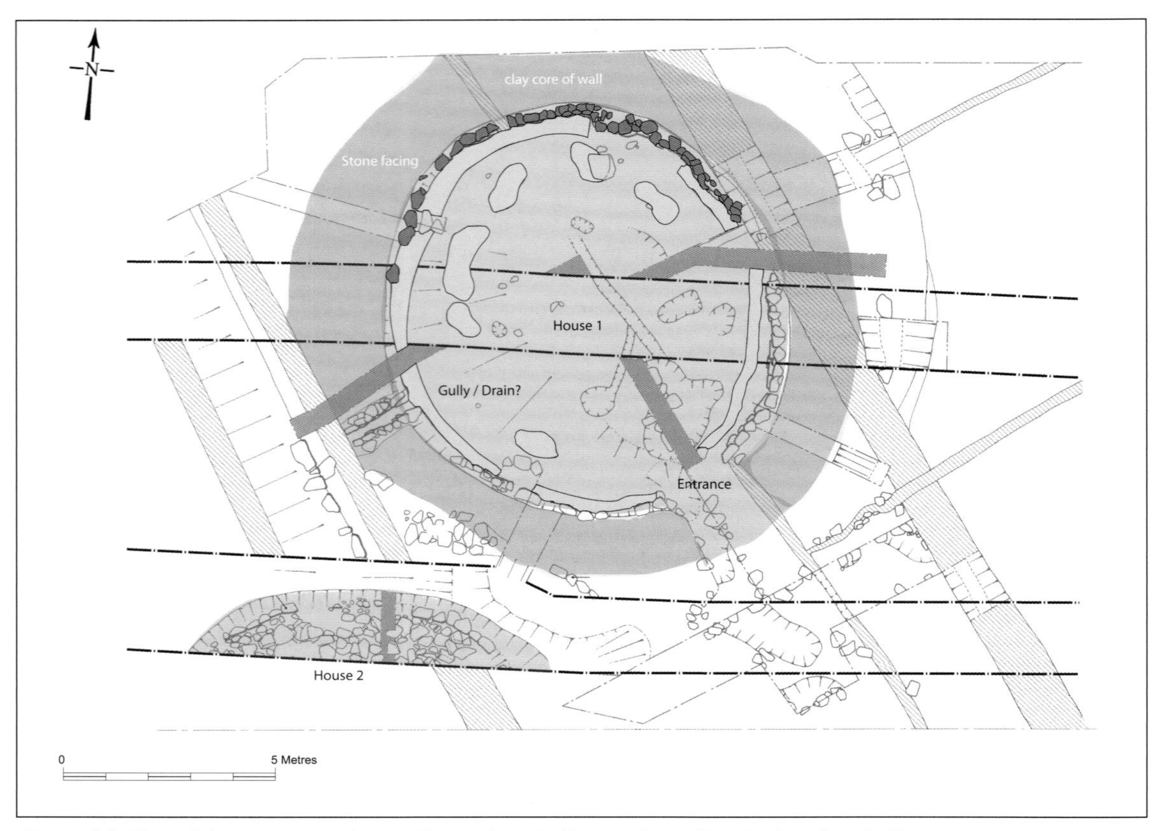

Figure 1.2 Plan of the Bronze Age house, House 1, at Ballyprior Beg (CFA Archaeology Ltd).

the roof. Nevertheless, the building and maintenance of the settlement took a lot of planning and thought. The result was structures that blended into the landscape, emphasising the people's closeness to nature.

The excavated roundhouse (Plate 1.2 and Figure 1.2) was circular in plan, 10m wide internally with a paved interior and a wall 2m thick which was stone faced with a clay core. These 'mass-walls' rely on weight and bulk, rather than technical sophistication, to achieve strength. They are also heat-efficient as they absorb solar heat during the day and transfer it to the interior at night, to the benefit of the occupants. The walls supported the roof, which was steeply sloping to shed the rain and to prevent the thatch becoming waterlogged. Wooden structures and thatched roofs are vulnerable to fire and it was clear that the house had burned down on at least one occasion. The paved entrance was in the south-east, facing the morning sun, and away from the worst of the wind and the rain. Outside there was a paved yard, where animals could be tethered, firewood stored, and crafts, like weaving or flint knapping practised in daylight hours.

Inside, the house would have been warm and dry. The excavation revealed a partially paved internal surface, with a drain around the perimeter at the base of the wall and this invites the possibility that there was a wooden floor to cover the drain. Wooden floors are known from crannog excavations but there is only circumstantial evidence from Ballyprior Beg. Aside from the advantages of below-floor air circulation, this suggestion stems from the unstructured nature of the excavated deposits and from the thousands of sharp flint chippings they contained. The latter would have been a hazard to unshod feet but would have been easily and safely lost below the floor. Further, it seems unlikely that the occupants lived on an island of midden material surrounded by an open drain. No direct evidence for the hearth was found, probably due to truncation, but a central warming stone hearth can be envisaged. Surviving internal furnishings consisted of large square stone seats and we may imagine the use of wooden furniture with the walls being covered perhaps with weavings or hides, although these have not survived.

The material evidence gives an insight into the daily lives of the occupants. Pottery vessels, made by hand-coiling were used for storage and cooking. Many of the cooking vessels had crusts of burnt food on them, either on the inside, or spilled down the outside. Although little bone survived due to the acidic clay, some evidence – mainly teeth – for cattle, sheep, pigs and dogs were recovered. We may also assume that deer were hunted and fish were caught though no direct evidence survived. Rounded beach or river stones were used for hammering purposes, such as flint tools and breaking bones to extract the marrow. Also in the house were large flat stones, pecked smooth on one side, used for the grinding of grain to make bread, but only three cereal grains were found. Flint is naturally found on Islandmagee, and it was an important and valued commodity in the past, one which could be traded or exchanged with merchants or other communities. The most commonly made tools were knives for cutting and scrapers for cleaning skins or debarking wood but the quality of the workmanship was, in general, low. Charcoal analysis suggests that the tree species on Islandmagee have changed little since the Bronze Age, with birch, oak and hazel being most common.

The most impressive finds from the site were a bronze axe and a lead-alloy hair ring, which resembles a Polo mint sweet in size and shape. Perhaps used to cut and shape the wood that built the settlement, the axe may have been brought out and displayed on special occasions when its exotic nature and metallic shine lent status and importance to its owner. The purpose of the hair ring is uncertain, but it is unusual in that most examples are made from gold, or are gold plated.

For reasons we don't understand, the people left the settlement and never returned, but as a final symbolic act, the axe was deliberately broken and buried in the centre of the house. Over the centuries, soil washed down the hillside covering the settlement, protecting it from view and preserving it. If it had not been for the electrical cable linking Scotland to Northern Ireland, it may never have been discovered.

Further reading

Suddaby, I. 2003 'The excavation of two Late Bronze Age roundhouses at Ballyprior Beg, Island Magee, County Antrim', *Ulster Journal of Archaeology* 62, 45–91.

A Bronze Age village at Corrstown, County Londonderry

Malachy Conway

A truly groundbreaking archaeological discovery was made in 2002 in the townland of Corrstown, to the south of Portrush. Today the fields, which once grew potatoes, contain over 200 new houses on the west side of Hopefield Road, but 3,500 years ago these fields were the site of a Bronze Age village, with the majority of the houses dating to the period 1500–1300 BC. At least 74 roundhouses were discovered during the excavation which ran for 10 months across an area of 22,200m^2 (Figure 1.3). This Bronze Age settlement did not represent the earliest human activity in the area as broken polished stone axes, made of local stone such as porcellanite and shale, numerous flint tools and fragments of handmade pottery dating to the Neolithic were also found. Some 2,000 years after the Bronze Age settlement was abandoned, occupation of the area

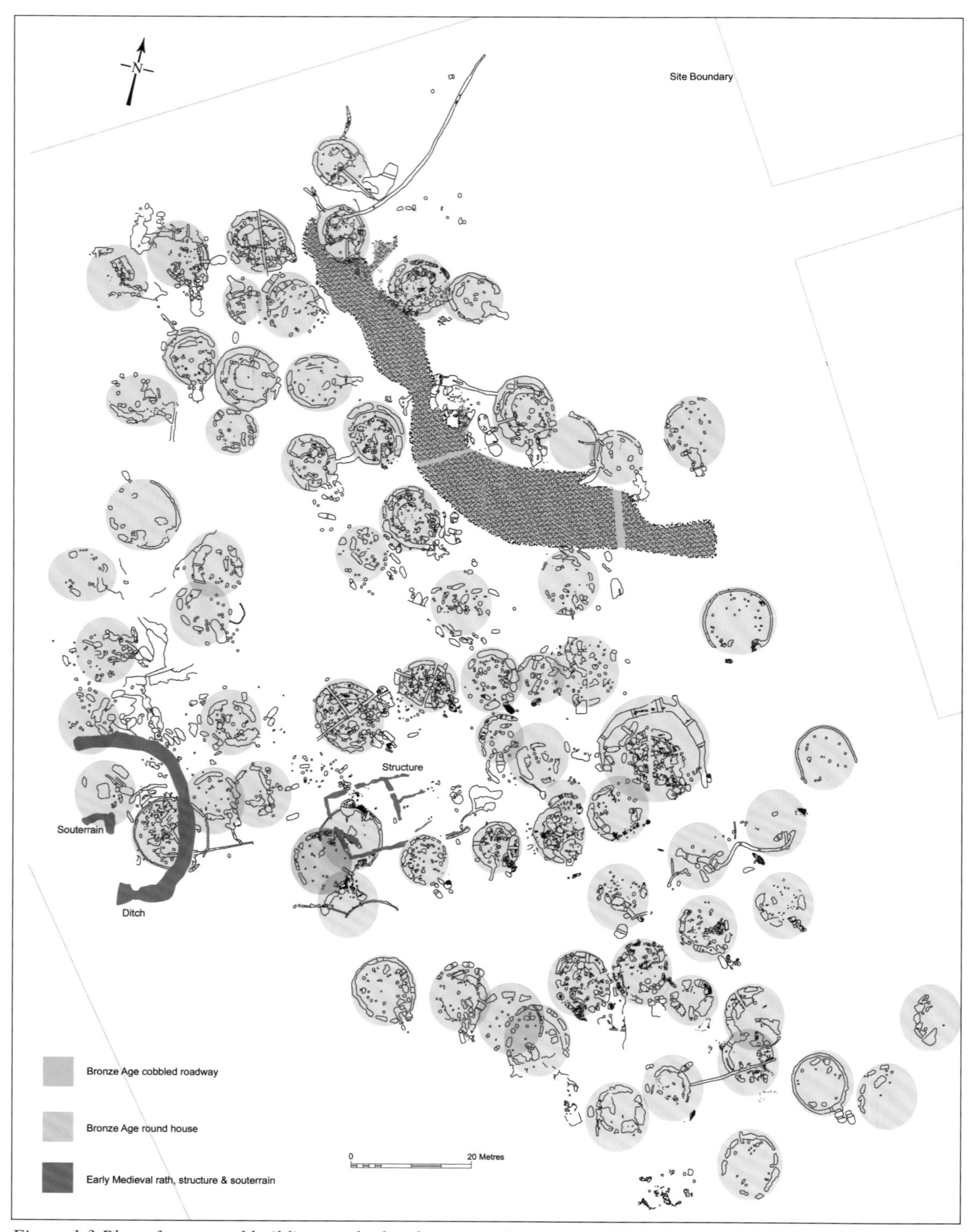

Figure 1.3 Plan of excavated buildings and other features at Corrstown (ACS Ltd).

resumed during the Early Medieval period when a ringfort and souterrain, and an unenclosed rectangular building were constructed on the site (Figure 1.3). The ringfort and souterrain were contemporary and dated to around AD 600–700, while the rectangular building was a later construction dating to around AD 850–900. The most significant discovery at Corrstown, however, was the remnants of the orderly village of roundhouses. Even today with well over 200 Bronze Age buildings so far recorded across the island, this remains an unparalleled discovery in the Irish archaeological record.

As the Corrstown site had been intensively farmed in modern times, the buried archaeological remains had been truncated, which meant that only the ground-plans of the Bronze Age houses survived. These comprised post-holes, pits, ditches and gullies which together represented the outlines of former buildings, not all of which were complete. Excavation in the area surrounding the houses revealed that it had been an 'open' settlement, as no evidence for any enclosing earthwork or palisade was found. The houses at Corrstown were located close together with several rows of houses surviving. In the few instances where structures overlapped this provided clear evidence that not all of the 74 roundhouses had been built or lived in at the same time and it is probable that somewhere in the region of 50 buildings were occupied at any one time.

A wide variety in both the size and plan of roundhouses was recorded. These ranged from small structures measuring 6.2m in diameter to larger buildings of up to 12m although most of the houses were roughly similar in size and between 7m and 9m in diameter. These are significantly smaller than many of our modern houses, but would still have provided an internal living area of around 20m^2 for the smaller buildings and up to 80m^2 for the larger ones. Clearly not all of the buildings served a domestic function and some would have been used as outbuildings for storage and possibly for farm animals. One construction method predominated and was recorded for 69 of the 74 houses excavated. These buildings were circular or oval in plan, delimited by a segmented external gully, and concentric within this lay an internal ring or double ring of post-holes. All of the houses had a single entranceway facing either to the south or south-east (Plate 1.3). Some of the structures also had an arrangement of post-holes at the entrance denoting the presence of an external porch.

Experiments in which archaeologists have reconstructed such houses, based on the results from excavations, can help us to explain and visualise how many of these structures were constructed, looked and even how long they lasted. The majority of the roundhouses at Corrstown had an internal ring of post-holes. These would have housed rounded upright timbers supporting a ring-beam on which radial rafters would have rested, meeting in the centre to form a conical-shaped roof. Horizontal timbers attached to the rafters would have braced the roof frame giving it additional structural strength and providing a base for the roof cladding of thatch, reeds or possibly sods. A roof of this type would have had a pitch of between 35° to 45° and extended almost to ground level. The segmented gullies around the buildings primarily acted as drip gullies channelling rain water away from the walls. Although surviving evidence was slight, it seems probable that a low wall of sods or stones (similar to that found at the Ballyprior Beg houses on Islandmagee) was built in the gap between the internal upright timbers and the drip gullies. Such a wall would have given additional support to the overhanging roof and provided extra insulation to the building.

The south or south-east facing entranceway is an important feature of the houses at Corrstown. Assuming the reconstruction described above is broadly correct, these houses would not have had any windows, thus the position of the doorways would have allowed the maximum amount of light and heat into the building. The southerly orientation also provided shelter from harsh northerly winds, especially when combined with a formal entrance porch.

Plate 1.3 Recording of one of the house sites at Corrstown (ACS Ltd). Note the entrance path to the building, bottom right.

The remains of finely cobbled paths were found outside many of the structures which formed laneways running along in front of the rows of houses. Several of the paths led directly onto a more prominent and heavily cobbled 'roadway' which passed through the site and which overlay and post-dated some earlier roundhouses (Figure 1.3). The road extended into the areas adjoining the excavation site suggesting that what was recorded at Corrstown was only a portion of an even larger settlement.

Few environmental remains such as seeds, grain and wood were recovered, which may in part be due to the intensive ploughing of the site in recent years, while the acidic soils mitigated against the survival of any animal bones. Only a small amount of burnt wood (alder) had survived within one building and a small quantity of barley (150 grains) in another. Evidence from other excavated sites where such environmental remains survive better (see Killymoon, Chapter 4) suggests that people in the Bronze Age practised a mixed farming economy, growing mostly barley along with other crops and keeping domestic livestock such as cattle, sheep and pigs. Few, if any, food preparation tools were found and the overall focus of the economy and diet of the people of this large Bronze Age settlement is still uncertain.

Other more durable finds, however, did survive. These included over 8,000 pieces of handmade pottery, mostly undecorated and of a bucket or urn shape. These broken potsherds represented over 400 individual pots. The remains of burnt residue on some of the fragments show that many of these vessels served as domestic cooking pots. The excavation also recovered over 16,000 pieces of flint and a large Gabbro macehead showing clearly that stone tool technology was still very much relied upon for daily use. No metal objects were found, but several stone moulds survived including part of a palstave axe mould and also several fragments of possible chisel moulds. Moulds such as these were a key component in the manufacturing process of bronze tools and weapons, but no other evidence was found for their production on site. One possible explanation for the absence of this type of evidence may be that due to the hazardous nature of metalworking with its potential to spread fire to domestic buildings, such production sites may have been intentionally located at a distance from the village. The high density of the settlement would also suggest that not all residents were involved in farming and food production. Non-food producers such as metalworkers would have relied on regular access to food, either through direct exchange with producers or through some form of market. This possibility of redistribution coupled with the scale and ordered layout of the site implies a certain degree of management and organisation.

Bell, bank and souterrain: excavations at Drumadoon, County Antrim

Cormac McSparron and Brian Williams

During the summer of 2002 the Centre for Archaeological Fieldwork, in conjunction with the NIEA, excavated a partially collapsed mound in the townland of Drumadoon in north County Antrim. Fresh erosion along one side exposed stonework early in the year, which led to the decision to excavate the site that summer and an excavation trench (17m by 8m) was opened across the top of the mound, covering almost the entire summit. The mound was believed to be the partial remains of an Anglo-Norman motte but excavations revealed that the motte, occupied in the thirteenth and fourteenth centuries AD, overlay a rath, which was constructed and in use between the eighth and tenth centuries AD, and which was built upon a natural gravel mound.

The rath and motte at Drumadoon were constructed on a gravel ridge, close to the village of Ballyvoy, and overlooking the Carey River to the south-west (Plate 1.4). An internally stone-faced earthen bank was initially constructed around the site possibly as early as the eighth century, with an entrance gap to the north-east. The bank survived to a height of approximately 1.5m, though it is likely that it would have originally been higher. Although at least half of the original rath has collapsed into the river valley, it is estimated that the bank would have enclosed a sub-circular area of about 20m in diameter. Immediately after the bank was constructed a souterrain, some 15.5m in length, was built. The souterrain was constructed by digging a large gully up to 2m deep into the ground, lining the sides with drystone walling and roofing it with lintel stones before covering it in earth and clay which concealed its location and formed the interior raised surface of the rath. It had two entrance passages, to the east and south-east, and a single chamber to the west. The chamber was isolated from the entrance passages by a creep – a constricted narrow and low portion of the souterrain. Assuming the souterrain, and in particular the chamber, was used as a place of refuge, the creep would have forced an assailant onto his hands and knees and he would have had to crawl to get access to those sheltering beyond. This would have allowed an easy dispatch of the vulnerable invader by an armed person in the refuge chamber.

Evidence was uncovered in the rath interior for two phases of occupation following the initial construction of the rath and souterrain. Radiocarbon dating has shown that these two phases of occupation occurred between the end of the eighth and the beginning of the tenth centuries AD. Immediately after the construction of the bank and souterrain, a hearth and paved area were built over the earth and clay deposits. These, along with the discovery of contemporary post-holes and stone wall footings, imply the existence of a house, although it was not possible to follow its exact footprint from the surviving remains. Located outside this probable house was a small, roughly circular, outhouse or grain store. It had been burnt down leaving the remains of charred wicker and thousands of charred cereal grains, mostly oats but with some barley also present. This is the

Plate 1.4 View of the collapsed mound (top left of photograph) at Drumadoon, from the Carey River valley, before excavation commenced (B. Hartwell).

first clear example of a grain store from an Irish rath excavation. In the second phase, a levelling deposit of earth was spread across the interior of the rath while a second hearth and paved area was constructed. Apart from these features no firm structural elements of buildings were found.

A large quantity of broken fragments of Souterrain Ware, a type of coarse pottery used for cooking and storage, was found within the souterrain and in the occupation layers and associated features. An iron spearhead and a copper-alloy fragment of a book mount were also found along with bones of cattle, sheep, pig, cod and seabream.

The rath was abandoned, probably in the years around or shortly after AD 900. It was not re-occupied until the middle of the thirteenth century when major reconstructions were undertaken to convert it into what was, in effect, a motte. The entrance into the rath was in-filled and the bank was partially destroyed. The top of the mound was also levelled and a new, but much lower, bank was built on top of this levelled surface. Bank material was used to level the interior of the site, in the process raising it by about 0.3m. It is likely that the site was then occupied by Anglo-Normans, though unfortunately this latest phase of occupation was badly disturbed by centuries of trampling by cattle and much of the evidence does not survive. Nevertheless, the stone footings of one light sub-circular structure did survive, which probably functioned as an ancillary structure of some sort rather than a house.

Finds and artefacts from this phase of occupation included late variants of Souterrain Ware and glazed English and other European-style pots, which were being imported into and manufactured in Ireland in the twelfth and thirteenth centuries. A silver halfpenny of Henry III, dating to the period 1247–1272, was also found from this phase along with iron tools and objects including a reaping hook, an awl or punch and several nails. Bones of cattle, sheep, horse, cod, saithe and seabream were all represented along with pieces of deer antler.

The most interesting artefact found in these thirteenth- to early fourteenth-century occupation deposits was a decorated copper-alloy bell shrine (Plates 1.5 and 1.6) which has been carefully studied by Cormac Bourke of the Ulster Museum. The shrine would originally have held a church bell which may have been used by, and consequently become the relic of, a saint. The side identified as the front of the shrine has a number of holes which are likely to be the attachment points of a, now missing, cross while on the back of the shrine, a cast figure of the crucified Christ with blue glass beads for eyes has been attached. The Christ figure has been identified by Bourke as having been manufactured at Limoges in France. On both the left and right faces of the bell shrine are sub-circular mounts for attaching a strap for suspending the shrine (Plate iii), which rests on four moulded feet. The manufacture of the shrine can probably be dated to the latter half of the twelfth century but the figure of Christ dates to the thirteenth century suggesting a later modification of the piece.

Plate 1.5 The Drumadoon bell shrine as it was found (CAF).

Plate 1.6 The bell shrine after cleaning and conservation (NIEA).

It is likely that Drumadoon was finally abandoned sometime before the end of the fourteenth century though the specific reason for the end of its use is unclear. Today the mound upon which Drumadoon is located has partly collapsed into the Carey River valley. If this had happened in the fourteenth century it could have led to the site's (very!) rapid abandonment. However, there are nineteenth-century accounts of the mound having been intact within living memory. It is possible that the site was abandoned because of political instability, perhaps resulting from strife amongst competing Anglo-Norman groups, which is documented for north Antrim between 1270 and 1280.

Alternatively its desertion may have been caused by the invasion in 1315 of Edward Bruce, brother of the King of Scots, in his attempt to expel the Anglo-Normans from Ireland. There is, however, no evidence of a Medieval assault on Drumadoon. Perhaps its owners were killed in battle elsewhere and the site was never re-occupied. Ultimately, however, as time passed Drumadoon, and sites like it, would have become militarily obsolete and increasingly unfashionable as places of residence. Continued occupation of these sites would have become progressively unlikely, although there was some occasional occupation of mottes into the fifteenth and even sixteenth century in Ireland. The finding of the bell shrine shows that the site came to a sudden end, whether by war, natural catastrophe or obsolescence. That an object of veneration such as the bell shrine was left there and not recovered shows that those responsible for it, and possibly Drumadoon itself, were for whatever reason, unable to retrieve it.

Further reading

McSparron, C. and Williams, B. 2009 'The excavation of an Early Christian rath with later medieval occupation at Drumadoon, Co. Antrim', *Proceedings of the Royal Irish Academy* 109C, 105–164.

The Movanagher village project: historical archaeology of the Ulster Plantation

Audrey Horning

In 1999 the Movanagher Village Project investigated the traces of an early seventeenth-century village established by the Mercers' Company of London as part of the Londonderry Plantation. Ill-fated from the start, Movanagher bawn and village – constructed between 1611 and 1618 on the western banks of the Bann north of Kilrea – attracted few permanent settlers and was abandoned following the 1641 Rebellion. Now a greenfield site, Movanagher presented archaeologists with an opportunity to address the material reflections of cultural interactions between English settlers and native Irish. Excavations focused upon the village site, unearthing evidence of both an English timber-framed house and an Irish dwelling occupied by settlers. The experimental use of geophysics, area sampling methods, a variety of artefact recovery techniques, and environmental analysis added a secondary research component to the project. Far beyond merely confirming the documentary record, archaeology on historic sites has the potential to not only inform but to radically alter understanding of the 'recent past' through examining documentary, material, ethnohistorical, and ethnographic data. While the political history of the Ulster Plantation era is well documented, understanding of the daily experiences of those communities and individuals caught up, willingly and unwillingly, in the process of enforced settlement is hazy at best. Informed archaeological research on sites such as Movanagher may be the only way to decipher the intricacies of a complex, formative period in the modern history of Ireland.

In the wake of the 1607 'Flight of the Earls', King James I worked to pacify the escheated counties of Armagh, Cavan, Coleraine, Fermanagh, Donegal, and Tyrone through the importation of loyal British subjects. The king coerced the livery companies of London into underwriting the venture, repaying them with grants of land in the newly created County Londonderry. As the premier of the 12 companies, the Mercers' Company was allocated 21,600 acres in two parcels: one along the Bann, and one in the forest of Glenconkeyne, west of Lough Neagh. The Company's main settlement was at the former, at Movanagher, strategically placed to exploit established salmon and eel fisheries near a Medieval ford. Building commenced in 1611 on the masonry bawn with sawmills and brick kilns hastily thrown up alongside the Bann. In 1619, the Movanagher settlement was described by Nicholas Pynnar in his survey of the Plantations as follows:

> "Castle formerly begun is now thoroughly finished, and is not inferior to any. A very large bawn, 120 ft. square, 4 flankers, of good stone and lime. Near the bawn are six houses of cagework, some covered with shingle, others thatched and inhabited by such poor men as they could find in the country, and these pay such dear rates for the land that they are forced to take Irish tenants to pay their rent. Diverse other houses of slight building, but far off, and dispersed in woods, where the inhabitants are forced to relieve such woodkerne as go up and downe the country."

A 1622 survey map by cartographer Thomas Raven (Figure 1.4) depicts a scattering of dwellings outside the bawn, with warehouses and a gristmill (that reportedly ruined grain) down by the river. The 1622 population on the Mercers' Proportion included 3 freeholders, 52 British men, and 145 native Irish. Even without any record of women or children, the clear majority were natives, not newcomers. The population imbalance and the surrounding landscape of dense forests and shadowy hills rendered Movanagher nearly indefensible. Anecdotal evidence for the destruction of the bawn during the 1641 Rebellion is recorded in the 1830s Ordnance Survey memoirs, while the Mercers' Company records contain a 1645 reference to the destruction of the castle. The ensuing Wars of the Three Kingdoms and the revocation of the Company's charter under Cromwell put paid to any restoration ideas.

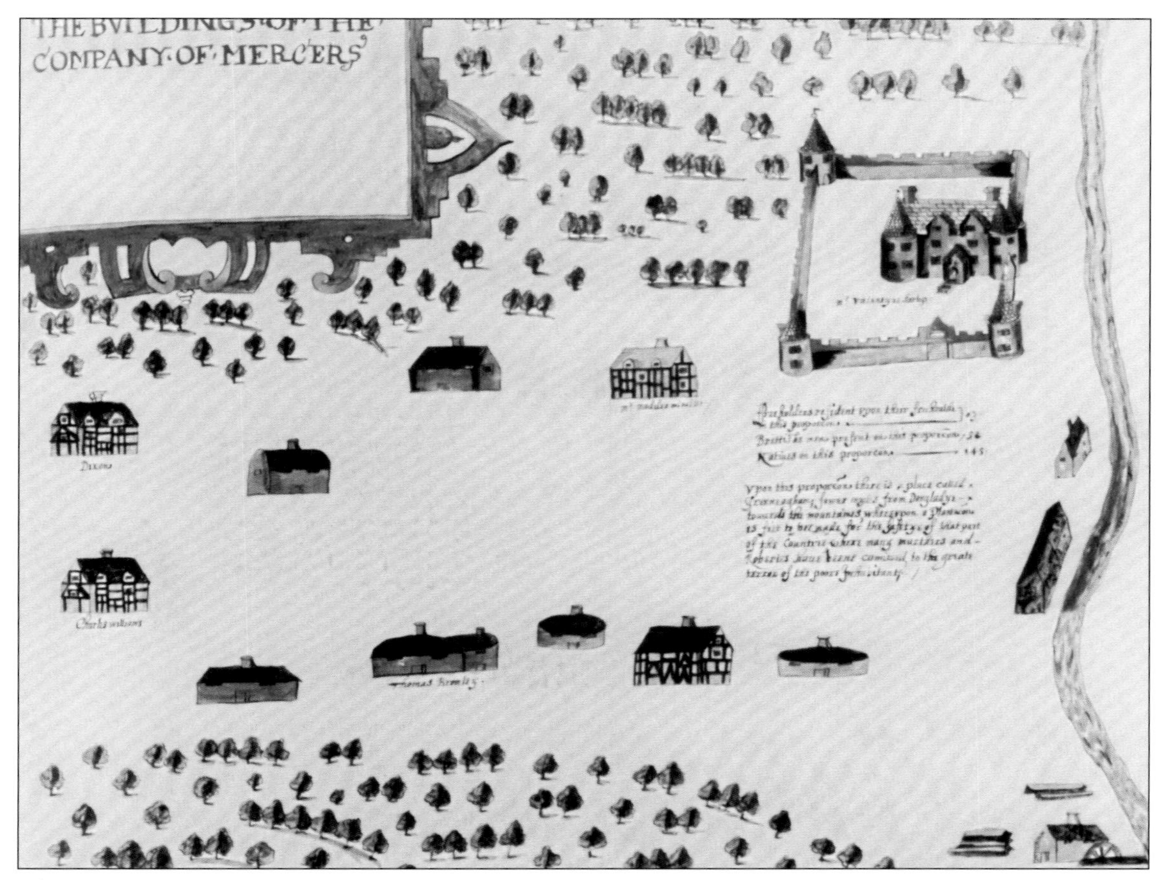

Figure 1.4 Thomas Raven's 1622 picture-map of Movanagher (A Plat of the Mercers Buildings) showing the bawn, different styles of houses and a warehouse and mill by the River Bann (reproduced courtesy of Lambeth Palace Library. Carew Manuscript: MS634 67v-68).

Unlike most of the London Company villages, Movanagher lacked a formal street plan. Consequently, an archaeological sampling strategy was devised to yield the maximum amount of spatial data. To detect areas of altered magnetism such as hearths and concentrations of brick, a magnetometer survey was conducted across the two fields extending south of the bawn. Anomalies were then 'ground-truthed' with archaeological trenches, but in general the geophysical prospecting effort was hampered by the underlying geology, characterised by basalt of volcanic origin which carries its own magnetic signature. In addition to a long trench (45m by 1.5m) situated to bisect several geophysical anomalies and provide a cross-section through the site, 50 small test trenches were sited at 10m intervals, each covering an area of 0.75m². On a ploughed site, artefact distributions derived from test pitting can be the most reliable indicator of subsurface features or activity areas. Experiments have demonstrated that while ploughed artefacts shift vertically, they remain in the same relative horizontal position.

All brick and slate unearthed in the test pits was retained, to hopefully pinpoint buried structures. One significant concentration of architectural material was identified near the south-eastern corner of the bawn, where test units yielded 20% of the recovered brick, measured by weight, and window glass and lead fragments. In contrast to assemblages found on Plantation-period urban sites, most Movanagher ceramics were coarse earthenwares. This zone, however, yielded English tin-enamelled earthenware, sometimes called delft, several sherds of Donyatt sgrafitto manufactured in Somerset, and Frechen stoneware from the Rhineland. The recovery of two musket balls from this locale – one flattened post-firing and the other rendered more deadly by being halved, served as a reminder of the precarious defensive position of the village. The 1622 Raven map depicts a large timber-framed structure, belonging to a Mr Madder Minister, in the locale of the artefact concentration. Typically, timber-framed houses were constructed atop timber, brick, or stone sills, placed on a levelled ground surface. The lack of a foundation trench means that structural evidence is readily ploughed away, thus the only surviving archaeological evidence for Mr Madder's house was the concentration of domestic and architectural artefacts unearthed in the plough soil.

Movanagher's architecture was not solely derived from English traditions. Raven noted the existence of "cabbins", and of the 10 structures he depicted, only 4 are timber-framed dwellings. Three others appear to be stone or earthen-walled, another sub-rectangular with an extension, while two are small and sub-rectangular. These two structures derive from a Late Medieval Irish vernacular tradition documented on maps, but previously unrecognised archaeologically. The physical evidence for one of the buildings depicted by Raven consisted only of a series of small, circular soil stains revealing an oval pattern of post-holes interspersed with stake-holes. The building measured approximately 4.3m by 6.1m, with a central open hearth (defined by an ashy layer) separating two rooms (Plate 1.7). The building incorporated earthfast posts presumably to carry a roof plate or trusses, while the small, driven posts interspersed between the timbers suggest that the walls were covered with a woven wattling plastered with daub. Traces of a cobbled yard and a fenced entry were uncovered on the south-eastern side of the structure. Artefacts from the post-hole fills, the pit, the occupation layer, and the cobbled surface support an early seventeenth-century date. Several fragments of English Border ware dating to around 1580–1610 were recovered, as were sherds of North Devon earthenware representing utilitarian forms such as milk pans and storage vessels. Accompanying these wares were numerous sherds of locally produced hand-built, Medieval Ulster coarse pottery cooking pots.

The mixing of Irish and English utilitarian wares associated with an Irish architectural form in an English settlement reflects a process of mutual accommodation and adaptation. Movanagher was heavily reliant upon local labour; for construction, to maintain the fisheries, and to provide much of the items traded at the Movanagher market, a market which shifted to Kilrea even before 1641.

Plate 1.7 UTV's Brian Black filming a piece to camera with Kilrea school children sitting around the hearth in one of the excavated vernacular houses at Movanagher. The upright bamboos mark the position of the excavated post- and stake-holes. The bawn wall is in the background (NIEA).

The complexity, and proximity, of the interactions between English and Irish in rural settlements such as Movanagher are difficult to codify, but are clearly reflected in the blend of material culture present archaeologically. In an isolated outpost whose inhabitants were described by Sir Nicholas Pynnar as "poor", and later as "the poorest men in all the country", economic levelling and the necessities of everyday life increased interaction and material accommodation. Material culture is not a direct reflection of ethnicity, but it does reflect a constant negotiation and renegotiation of identity, often at a subconscious level. While religious differences and proffered identities ensured intolerance, hostility, and legislated separation, individuals were irrevocably changing by way of their shared experiences. This process was rooted at the bottom of the socio-economic ladder and marked in communities located at places like Movanagher where the business of the day for both natives and newcomers was not political, but chiefly practical.

Further reading

Horning, A.J. 2001 'Dwelling houses in the Old Irish barbarous manner: archaeological evidence for Gaelic architecture in an Ulster Plantation village'. In, P. Duffy, D. Edwards, and E. FitzPatrick (eds), *Gaelic Ireland: land, lordship, and settlement*, 375–396. Dublin: Four Courts Press.

Horning, A.J. 2007 'On the banks of the Bann: the riverine economy of an Ulster Plantation village', *Historical Archaeology* 41(3), 94–114.

Horning, A.J. 2007 'The archaeology of British expansion: Ireland and North America in the seventeenth century'. In, A. Horning, R. Ó Baoill, C. Donnelly, and P. Logue (eds), *The post-medieval archaeology of Ireland, 1550-1850*, 51-70. Dublin: Wordwell.

CHAPTER 2

Public Space and Architecture

Chapter 2: Public Space and Architecture

Introduction

A mixed bag of sites have been brought together in this chapter; Bronze Age stone circles, Neolithic and Iron Age monumental timber buildings, as well as seventeenth-century formal gardens. What they all have in common is that they were designed for non-utilitarian use, were executed on a large scale, required a huge investment of materials and labour, and had, and in some cases continue to have, a significant influence on the surrounding landscape.

The use of the term architecture in the title is deliberate. The accounts of the ceremonial timber structures at Ballynahatty and Navan Fort (see below in this chapter) encourage us to approach both of these monuments as they were originally conceived – as grand timber buildings. The same problems, however, are presented here as in the previous chapter, as although we are dealing with structures on a very different scale, only the ground plans of the buildings survive.

Archaeological investigations have uncovered the foundations of lost timber buildings at both Ballynahatty and Navan Fort. The regular layout and dimensions of the post-holes uncovered at both sites suggest that the people who built these structures set about the task with a preconceived design. What this concept was, we can only now imagine; the gaps between the large timber posts may have been left open or filled in with some form of walling; the timbers may have been carved, painted or embellished in some other way; and they may or may not have supported a roof or perhaps just a series of lintels.

The scale of these constructions and the necessary labour to prepare and transport each of the timbers used indicates a massive investment by the local communities that built them. The size of these monuments and their prominent hilltop locations made them highly visible and a focus for the surrounding landscape. This physical presence along with the presumed involvement of large numbers of people to create them, suggest major community ventures.

But was this community involvement willing or unwilling and can the timber structures at Ballynahatty and Navan Fort, along with the stone circles at Copney (see below in this chapter), all be considered as 'public' monuments? Studies have shown that public architecture, buildings and planned spaces, typically emerge in societies where there is increased affluence. They are also often deemed to carry an idea of national identity. Such societies are also, in most cases, hierarchical and it seems probable that these structures, whether they were religious or secular, functioned in the same ways as modern temples, churches, civic and judicial buildings. These modern buildings are all ostensibly open to the public, but access to, and within, them is strictly controlled, with public and private quarters. The authors' imagining of how people interacted with the built components at Ballynahatty, Navan Fort and Copney all envisage communal gatherings but with certain restrictions on physical and visual access.

The public architecture, buildings and planned spaces of prehistoric communities can be viewed as a reflection of the belief systems and contemporary culture, with the structures arising out of a desire to express certain ideals. It seems likely that Copney and Ballynahatty had a religious rather than a secular role given the association of human remains. Navan Fort has been identified as one of the regional capitals in the Iron Age although excavations have suggested that the site was a religious sanctuary in the Early Iron Age and possibly used for kingship ceremonies in subsequent centuries. To these we could add the passage tombs at Ballynahatty and the ring-ditches and four-poster structures at Ballintaggart (see Chapter 6) as, although these served as tombs, it is probable that they were also the focus for communal gatherings and ritual activities. These excavated sites also form only one component of what might be described as ritual landscapes in which other non-domestic structures and monuments are located.

Our understanding of early religion and culture is poor though it seems likely that the observation of the cycles of life (birth, puberty, marriage and death) and celebration of significant times in the year, in particular the solstices and equinoxes marking the changing seasons, were the focus of gatherings, celebrations and rituals. The latter is suggested by certain monuments, including Ballintaggart and Copney, where possible astronomical alignments have been proposed. We can only imagine what these gatherings involved; processions, perhaps dancing and singing, while the light from the changing day- or night-sky would have made a significant contribution to the ambience and character of these events. Feasting may also have been part of the ceremonies – as suggested by the recovery of animal bones at Ballynahatty. Alternatively, the consumption of food and drink may have been carried out elsewhere, maintaining a division between the realms of the dead and the living.

In early Christian times the Church and its ordained members inherited this role and administered the celebrations of births, deaths and marriages, marked the annual festivities of Easter and Christmas and the multitude of saints' feast days, as well as the daily and weekly ecclesiastical observations. A glimpse of the pageantry and spectacle of the Church is provided by two recently rediscovered shrines: the highly ornate Clonmore shrine (see Chapter 3) and the Drumadoon bell shrine (see Chapter 1). To those who saw them in Early Medieval times, these must have seemed remarkable and been regarded with wonder and reverence. The two shrines were also designed to be suspended by a chain or strap facilitating their transportation, presumably during processions, thus presenting a further intimation of the nature of celebrations at the time.

The formal gardens of Lisburn Castle, described in this chapter, present a very different monument. The grounds were laid out as pleasure gardens for the exclusive use of a small number of people. The fortunes of the gardens and their owners changed over subsequent decades and at the turn of the twentieth century the gardens were bequeathed to Lisburn town. What had therefore begun life as a private, designed landscape to be enjoyed by a few, has now been transformed into a public monument and a celebrated feature of the modern city. The manor house which the gardens originally accompanied no longer survives, thus the setting and context of the gardens have changed. This typifies an aspect of all of the monuments discussed in this chapter – they have outlasted the societies that created them and survive and are reused in a changing landscape.

Prehistoric ritual at Ballynahatty, County Down

Barrie Hartwell

At the end of the last Ice Age the retreating glaciers deposited a thick layer of sands, gravels and boulders on the broad floor of the Lagan Valley. Fast flowing rivers eroded and dissected this material and one of the results can be seen in the townland of Ballynahatty where an isolated plateau sits on the east bank of a loop of the River Lagan, just 6km south of the centre of present day Belfast. For over 1,000 years, until about 2500 BC, this progressively became the focus of one of the most intensive ritual landscapes in the north of Ireland. Location was crucial – set apart in the Lagan Valley yet accessible both from the coast and the interior, and also to people moving from north to south, fording the Lagan at nearby Shaw's Bridge.

Today, Ballynahatty is the location of the impressive remains of a Late Neolithic henge monument – the Giant's Ring. At 200m in diameter and 4m high, it is perhaps the best surviving example of this type of ceremonial enclosure in Ireland. At its centre sits an altogether older monument, a megalithic passage tomb, and scattered through the fields to the north and west are flat cemeteries, a standing stone, tombs, cists and ring-barrows, both levelled and revealed by the plough when the land was enclosed in the eighteenth and nineteenth centuries. A large boulder sitting at the end of a short ridge in the field just 100m to the north-west of the henge may be a remnant of this ritual landscape. However, around 2500 BC, this ridge was the location of one of the finest examples of Neolithic architecture in Ireland – a timber 'temple' that dominated the plateau. This was the subject of 10 seasons of excavation, until 2000, by Queen's University Belfast (QUB) supported by the NIEA, and with the kind permission of the landowner, Jim Thompson of Ballylesson.

The passage tombs provided an original focus of ritual in this Neolithic landscape. The existing tomb at the centre of the Giant's Ring now consists of a chamber with a short passage and entrance to the west. Originally it would have been surrounded by a kerb of stones retaining a covering mound of earth. Nineteenth-century accounts record similar monuments in Ballynahatty and the QUB excavations found evidence of five smaller versions with their characteristic Carrowkeel Ware pottery containing human cremations. Early in the third millennium BC, at great physical cost, an enormous earthen bank was dug from an internal quarry trench around the old passage tomb. This henge monument (the Giant's Ring), provided at once an elevated platform and grandstand where activities could be openly observed within, but it also enforced social division and exclusion. Were those workers who built the monument willing contributors to the enterprise, motivated perhaps by religious zeal, or were they coerced? Either way, this was the product of a hierarchical society.

The timber ritual complex was built after the henge and was first seen in 1989 as a crop mark in aerial photographs (Plate 2.1). The complex can be divided into four units (Figure 2.1): the large

Plate 2.1 Aerial photograph of the Ballynahatty crop marks taken during the exceptionally dry summer of 1989. The bank of the Giant's Ring can be seen at the top right (B. Hartwell).

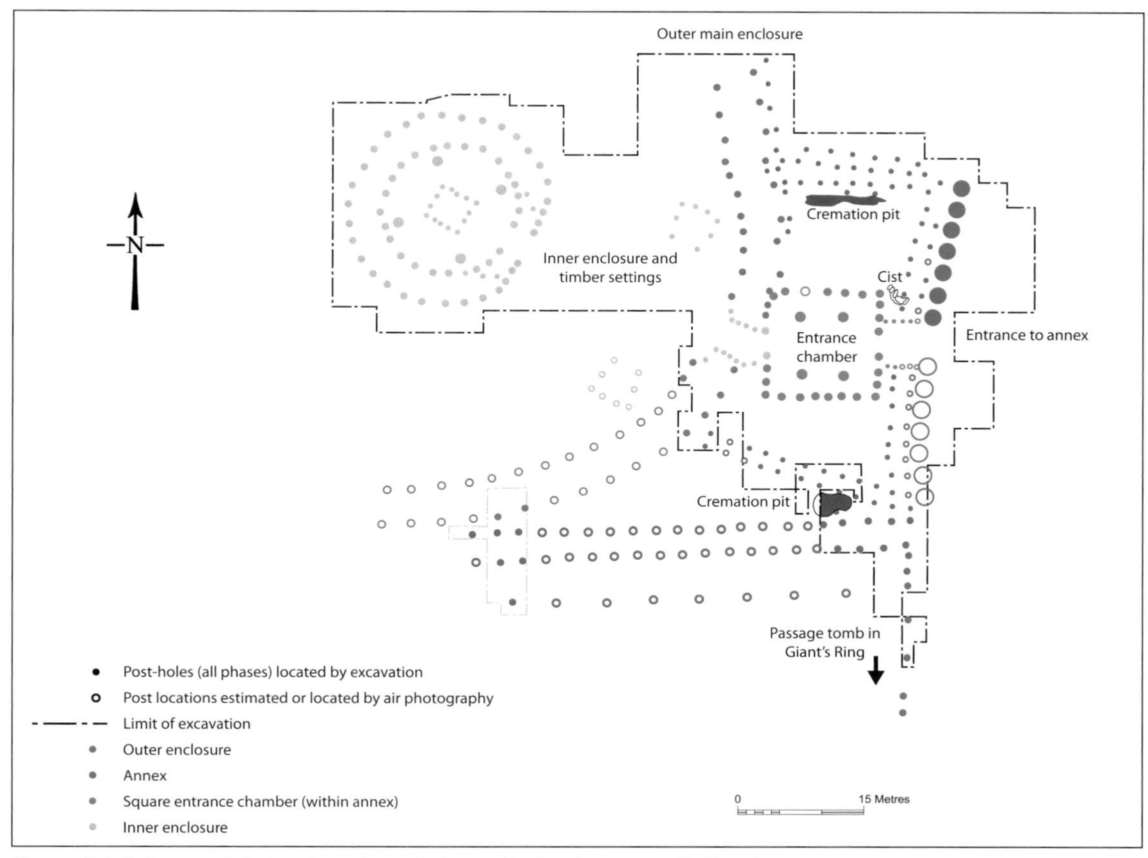

Figure 2.1 Colour-coded site plan of post-holes and other features at Ballynahatty.

outer enclosure, 70m by 100m, carefully placed on the edge of the ridge; an annex appended to the east end which controls entry; the square entrance chamber within the annex; and at the centre of the whole complex, a 16m-diameter inner enclosure with a square central platform and outer timber settings. The aerial photographs and excavations showed the complex to consist of over 400 post-holes, mostly dug to a depth of over 2m. They would have held a variety of free-standing posts between 4m and 8m in height and 0.2m to 1.2m in diameter, the taller ones requiring a ramp to pivot the post into the hole. Experiments have shown that each post-hole and its accompanying ramp would have taken 25 hours to dig with an antler pick. To cut down each tree and trim the branches using polished stone axes, then drag the timber onto the site, down the ramp, haul it upright and backfill the hole would have taken considerably longer. A conservative estimate for just the erection of the posts comes to 13,000 hours of work. Manufacture of the axes and the rope, the initial site clearance, the preparation of a planked façade to the inner enclosure, and possible lintels would easily have trebled this. This was a major intervention in the landscape conceived on a grand scale and requiring considerable planning and organisation of resources. The plan is so sophisticated that it suggests a fully evolved, architect-designed response to established rituals.

Excavation has provided us with a blueprint of the foundations indicating an exceptional building – but not a domestic one. This is public building in the grand style, elegantly designed to control space, views and access to an inner sanctum containing a platform structure (Plate 2.2 and Figure 2.2). In the context of the later Neolithic, this may have been used as an exposure platform

Plate 2.2 The inner enclosure at Ballynahatty after excavation (B. Hartwell).

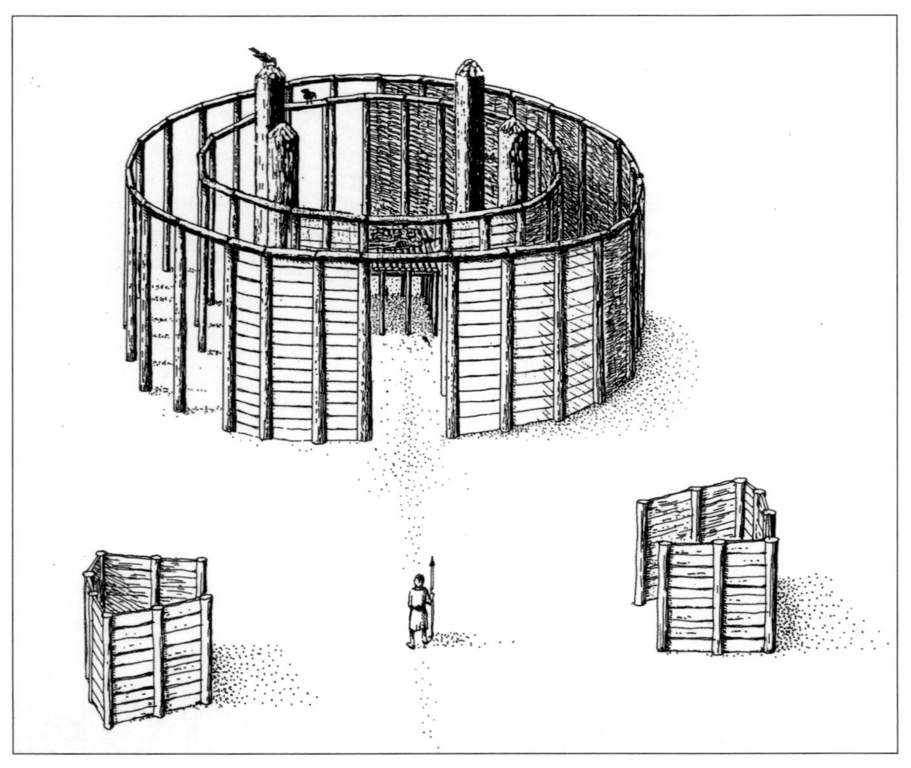

Figure 2.2 Reconstruction drawing of the inner enclosure, or 'temple', at Ballynahatty by Barrie Hartwell.

for excarnation. If we carefully mix fact and inference with speculation we can reconstruct how this ritual structure – the 'temple' - may have functioned.

Access was from the east end of the ridge through a line of massive timber posts. Imagine a small procession of family members carrying a body on a bier and labouring up the slope – the ominous façade, with its narrow entrance, towers above, obscuring the main enclosure behind. Once through this entrance a short passage leads into a square entrance chamber. This seems to be a stopping point, perhaps for extended rituals. We know it was an important area because it is marked by four taller posts so that the location of this part of the ceremony can be seen from outside. The body is set here while further activities take place in the annex – pottery, flint and some pig bone found on either side suggest feasting – perhaps a celebration of the life of the dead relative. From the entrance chamber, the view forward into the inner enclosure misses the elaborate internal structures where the gruesome finale takes place. The family stays in the annex, forbidden to go further and unable to witness the next stage because the architect has carefully angled the alignment of the inner enclosure so that it is obscured from the entrance. The tall timbers throughout the temple block all views but those of the sky and the passageway.

Continuing, the priests process with the corpse through the next passage, which is the entrance to the main inner enclosure. Only now, turning towards the right, is the inner temple revealed, but just 9m further a critical point is reached. To the left and right the wedge-shaped, eastern settings of posts are laid out on a circle with a curved back and converging sides (Figure 2.1). Only from this central point can the entire contents of both these structures be seen – piles of human bones show that these are the homes of the ancestors. Moving forward, the line is crossed into their realm. Straight ahead is the smaller inner temple with its narrow entrance through a planked timber façade (Figure 2.2). From this point the platform at the centre can be seen in its entirety. If the eastern settings contain generations of bones, the excarnation platform is where the corpse will be defleshed. The position of this significant area is again marked by four taller posts so that the location can be identified from outside. Carrion birds sit on the posts waiting for their next meal, decomposing bodies heave with maggots and the air is filled with the buzzing of flies and the odour of putrefaction. But out of this decaying flesh the bones will eventually emerge, washed by the rain and bleached by the sun. This is where human identity literally falls away and the individual moves into the parallel world of the ancestors. The inner temple, open to the skies, is the conduit whereby the dead are propelled into collective anonymity and eternity.

The real story is certainly more complex than this. A pit on the south side of the annex is full of charcoal and contains traces of human and animal bone and cereal grain. The annex itself was enlarged to look even more impressive from the south. Why were some people cremated and others not? What took place in the remainder of the outer enclosure? And what eventually happened to the temple complex? We can at least go some way to answering this last question.

The base of one of the oak posts seems to have rotted below ground level so perhaps the temple complex was in existence for 50–100 years or more, but for much of the site the evidence points to the structure having been deliberately burnt. Below ground the posts should have remained intact. Instead they were systematically dug or pulled out and charcoal and stones poured back into the holes. The superstructure was transformed from corruptible wood into a permanent state – charcoal. In effect, it was treated like a human body – it was cremated.

Aerial photography suggests that the complex may have been matched by another timber temple surrounding the passage tomb within the existing Giant's Ring. So we may have duality here, the temple on the ridge reaches towards the sky and below it another temple focuses on the tomb and the passage into the earth.

By 2500 BC the Ballynahatty plateau was steeped in over 1,000 years of religious ritual. A line of timbers ran south from the great entrance façade of the timber temple directly towards the founding passage tomb to complete the cycle of monuments. Thus, each new site had been integrated with the previous one and the ritual landscape was developed and enhanced.

This then, is Ballynahatty, and in the grand finale, the timber temples were razed in a massive conflagration and consigned to the world of the ancestors. These monuments have survived for over 4,500 years, proclaiming ancient rights, rituals and territorial aspirations, an enduring symbol of the ancestral heartland of the Neolithic farmers of the Lagan Valley and their enigmatic religion.

The phenomenon of Copney stone circles

Claire Foley

The stone circle complex at Copney, County Tyrone (Plate 2.3) is one of the best examples of a ceremonial site of the Early Bronze Age in Ireland and probably dates to between 2000 and 1500 BC. The stones were first reported in 1979 by local historians, although the archaeological potential of the site had been known to the landowners through peat-cutting, with quiet speculation for many generations. The circles are situated on gently sloping ground to the north side of Copney Hill in the Sperrin foothills, between Omagh and Cookstown. The site forms part of the wider group of mid-Ulster stone circles found in the uplands of Counties Tyrone, Londonderry and Fermanagh. These are typically characterised by circles of low upright stones or orthostats, 0.1m to 0.5m high, found singly or in pairs, and are often associated with linear alignments of similarly low stones tracking in various directions.

When Copney was first surveyed in the 1980s very few stones were discernible above the mantle of blanket peat which had grown over the abandoned site from about 1200–1500 BC. Using probes to find the buried orthostats, nine stone circles ranging from 6m to 20m in diameter were recorded as well as a stone alignment and a cairn. The most prominent feature of the site is a distinctly anthropomorphic-looking standing stone nearly 2m in height, which seems to be positioned to dominate the series of stone circles running downhill from west to east.

In 1994, with the opportunity of an exceptionally dry summer, it was decided to begin the process of removing the peat cover to present the site for visitors, as the landowners had kindly given the site into State Care. Until the peat removal it was assumed that each of the circles would be defined by low, well-spaced stones, similar to the designs of other stone circles known in the region. There was just a hint of an internal arrangement of stones, a phenomenon displayed elsewhere in the 'dragon's teeth' of the Beaghmore stone circles some 11km to the north-east. There was, however, little expectation of the complex monument which was revealed.

Two stone circles and part of a third were exposed and this, coupled with the extensive probing that was carried out, provides a good understanding of the overall shape of the site. Other elements of the site remain peat-covered for their ongoing protection. The newly exposed stones were presented as startlingly white, bleached from immersion in the acidic peat for over 3,000 years. This environment had caused the stone surfaces to break down and the result was that soon after excavation, many of the stones began shedding particles like sugar onto the basal peat below. A geological study carried out by Queen's University Belfast identified the stone type as andesitic porphyry, an unusual metamorphic rock, available as bedrock in the immediate vicinity. Now, following several years of exposure since the 1994 excavations, the surfaces of the majority of stones have stabilised and also reverted to their more muted natural colouring.

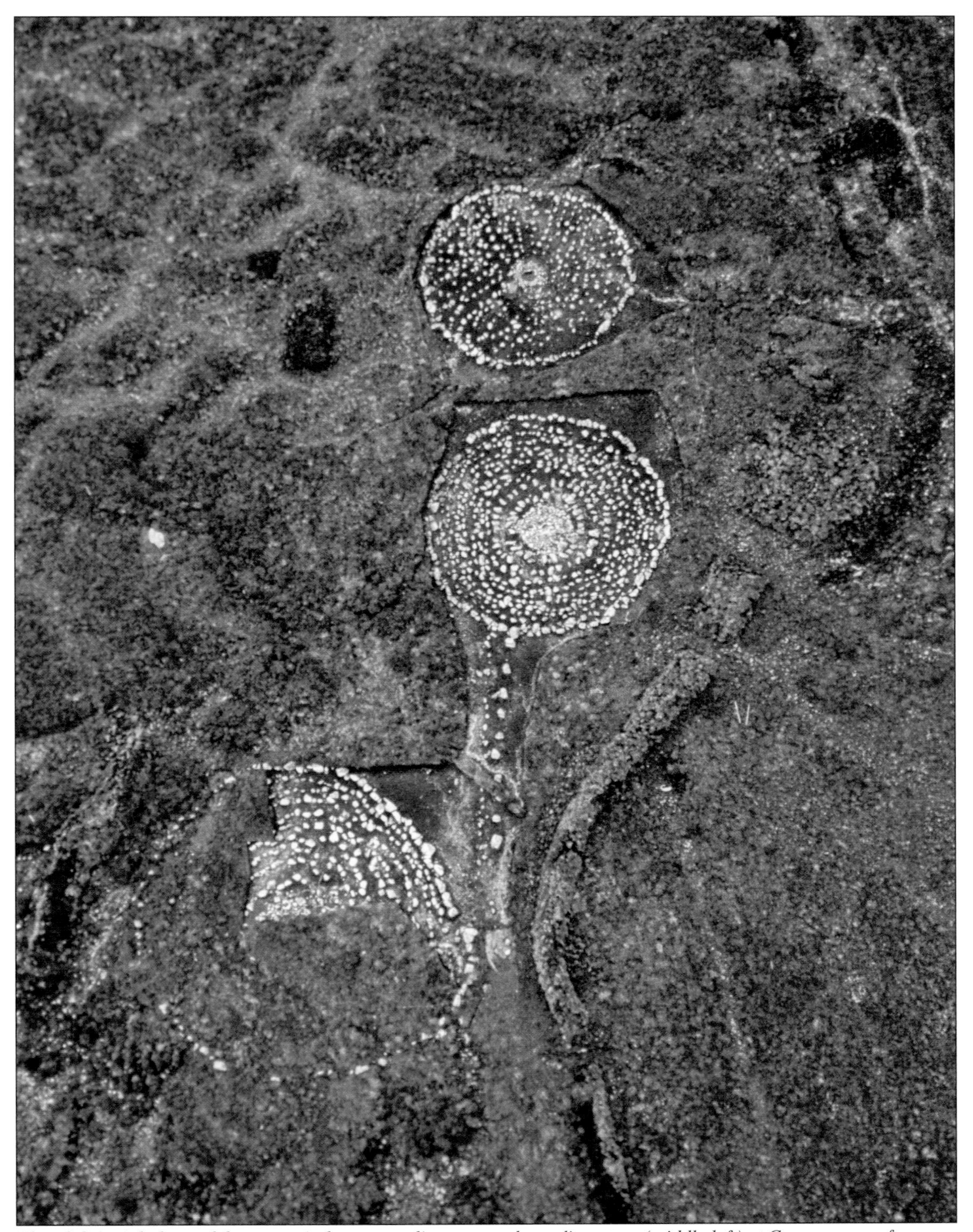

Plate 2.3 Aerial photo of the stone circles, stone alignment and standing stone (middle left) at Copney soon after their excavation in 1994 (NIEA). The photo is orientated approximately north-south.

Copney is unusual among the mid-Ulster group of stone circles in a number of ways. The perimeters of the Copney circles are tightly packed with contiguous stones: elsewhere they are usually spaced apart. The areas enclosed by the orthostats of the Copney circles are also peppered with hundreds of small uprights in contrast to the open spaces surrounded by other circles in the group. Here stones are set radially in one circle (Plate 2.4) and concentrically in two others. Movement would have been difficult in the Copney stone circles and they were probably intended to be observed from without.

Plate 2.4 One of the two fully excavated stone circles with the internal small upright stones set radially within the outer perimeter (NIEA).

At the centre of each of the three exposed circles a cairn of small stones was found, each with a central cist lying open and a displaced capstone lying close by. While these best resemble burial cairns, no human remains or grave goods were found in association with any of them. Their open presentation suggests that they were robbed either in antiquity or in long forgotten peat-cutting.

A double alignment of stones forming a stone row, running east-west, projects radially from the second stone circle at the top of the hill and joins the edge of the third circle at a tangent. The purpose of such alignments is not immediately obvious but they are common in this mid-Ulster series of stone circles. Theories abound about astronomical observation at such sites. They may have functioned in marking a particular sunrise, sunset, moon rise or possibly some less obvious event of movements of planets or stars. People then, as now, would have viewed the night sky with curiosity and awe realising the daily and seasonal variations in positions of heavenly bodies. Perhaps such sites were a response to observed events like comets or meteor showers and an expression of solidarity to impress or appease imagined gods who might be thought to be observing from the sky. Early agriculturalists will have been conscious of subtle variations in climate causing crops to thrive or fail from one year to the next.

The community responsible for these circles, whether they were built all at once or over a longer period of time, evidently had a clear sense of belonging to a particular cultural group with ideas in common with people across a wide geographic territory. The site is perhaps a physical expression of Bronze Age society beliefs and spiritual aspirations and it clearly conforms to a previously known architectural canon. It took effort and design knowledge to create and we can only guess that it was used for important ceremonies which may have been related to the fertility of the farmland. The creation of a 'sacred' space on this now remote hillside will have meant excluding this area from cultivation or grazing, the sacrifice of a stretch of potentially open farmland. It will have served as a public, focal point for Early Bronze Age inhabitants in this immediate locality and beyond.

This site illustrates a sophistication of ceremonial thought and purpose by a community in Tyrone over 3,000 years ago. While it is unusual in many aspects and excellently well preserved, it is part of a cultural expression which was widespread in north-western Europe at the time. Stone circle ceremonial sites of tall stones occur in some profusion in Cork and Kerry with occasional examples further east and north in counties Wicklow, Mayo and Donegal. Dramatic stone circles are also found in Scotland, Cumbria, Wales, Somerset, Cornwall and Brittany. Only in mid-Ulster, where there are upwards of 120 examples, do they find expression in such low-stature, as here at Copney. This may suggest that the complexes were indeed designed to be seen from the heavens and that the overall shape was the critical issue with no particular relevance in the height of the stones. Whatever their purpose, we are fortunate that they have survived in an area of sustainable farming where turf-cutters and grazing animals have availed of nature's bounty side by side for thousands of years without damaging the archaeological site beneath their feet.

Navan Fort as a public monument

Chris Lynn

Navan Fort is a large prehistoric earthwork enclosure on a drumlin 2km west of Armagh City (Plate 2.5). It was built some 700 years before written records began in Ireland, but could traditions recorded about the site in the early historic period have some basis in fact? The Early Medieval tales known as the Ulster Cycle consistently portray the site, then called Emain Macha, as the headquarters of a warrior elite, presided over by a king with his attendants, champions and chief druid. According to the tales the king had a royal hall at Emain Macha for feasting and entertainment and the place was used for musterings by the Ulster warriors prior to battles.

The picture thus presented is of a site with public architecture in the manner of an Early Medieval chiefdom. It has been suggested that the tales mainly transmit a picture of society at the time they were composed and written down in the Early Medieval period. Archaic sections are seen as guesses as to what the past might have been like, in some cases informed by Classical sources and the Bible. Other scholars have suggested that the portrayal of Emain Macha and its associated personages in the tales may provide some genuine evidence for life and society in later prehistory.

The interpretations have had to be revised because archaeological investigations at Emain Macha, which started in 1961, have shown that, far from being a royal palace and military encampment, the site was a religious sanctuary in the Early Iron Age. The ceremonial significance of the place seems to be overlooked, perhaps deliberately, in the tradition that has come down to us. Nevertheless, we can point to several things that the ancient tradition may have got right: the date of the monuments at Navan Fort/Emain Macha; the prestige of the site in later prehistory; the association of the monuments with upper levels of society (royal or religious) and the presence of large and unusual wooden buildings.

Excavation of a circular-plan embanked earthwork (Site A – Plate 2.5) on the Navan hilltop was begun in 1961. It was thought that this might be a small rath and the question was why an

Plate 2.5 Aerial photo of Navan Fort with the large mound, Site B, located on the hilltop to the right and Site A to the left of it (NIEA).

ordinary looking settlement of the Early Medieval period was built inside a large and prestigious prehistoric monument? The excavation demonstrated that it was a prehistoric ring-barrow, which had been built over the site of an even earlier structure, a large circular-plan 'house' 20m in diameter. This find demonstrated for the first time the existence of large, evidently prestigious, prehistoric wooden buildings at the site. Its discovery contributed to the decision two years later to begin excavation of the main monument on the Navan hilltop.

Between 1963 and 1971 the most prominent monument, a large mound (Site B), was entirely removed through excavation and an extraordinary sequence of events was revealed. First, the builders had erected a large round building of four concentric rings of large, upright, oak posts, some 280 in all, surrounded by a timber wall 40m in diameter (Figure 2.3). The building (known to archaeologists as 'the 40m structure'), may have had an openwork superstructure and was dominated by a large post at its centre. This was the trunk of an oak tree, the butt of which was preserved in its socket in the ground, by the dampness of the subsoil. The mound builders had then heaped stones inside the building to form a flat-topped cairn, the base of which was held in place against the inside of the wall of the timber building (Plate 2.6). After this, the wooden structure was deliberately set on fire. Its remains may then have been cleared away: apart from burnt kindling and the charred remnants of its outer wall no other remains of the outside or roof of the structure were found. The cairn and the rings of unburnt oak posts it encased were subsequently covered by layers of turves and soils to form the 5m-high mound that survived down to the 1960s when it was excavated (and subsequently restored). It is clear that, whatever its components were meant to represent, the mound was built to be a permanent monument and to have a function in the future.

There has been much speculation about the purpose of this strange monument. At least we know from tree-ring dating of the central post that the 40m structure was erected in 95 BC. Further

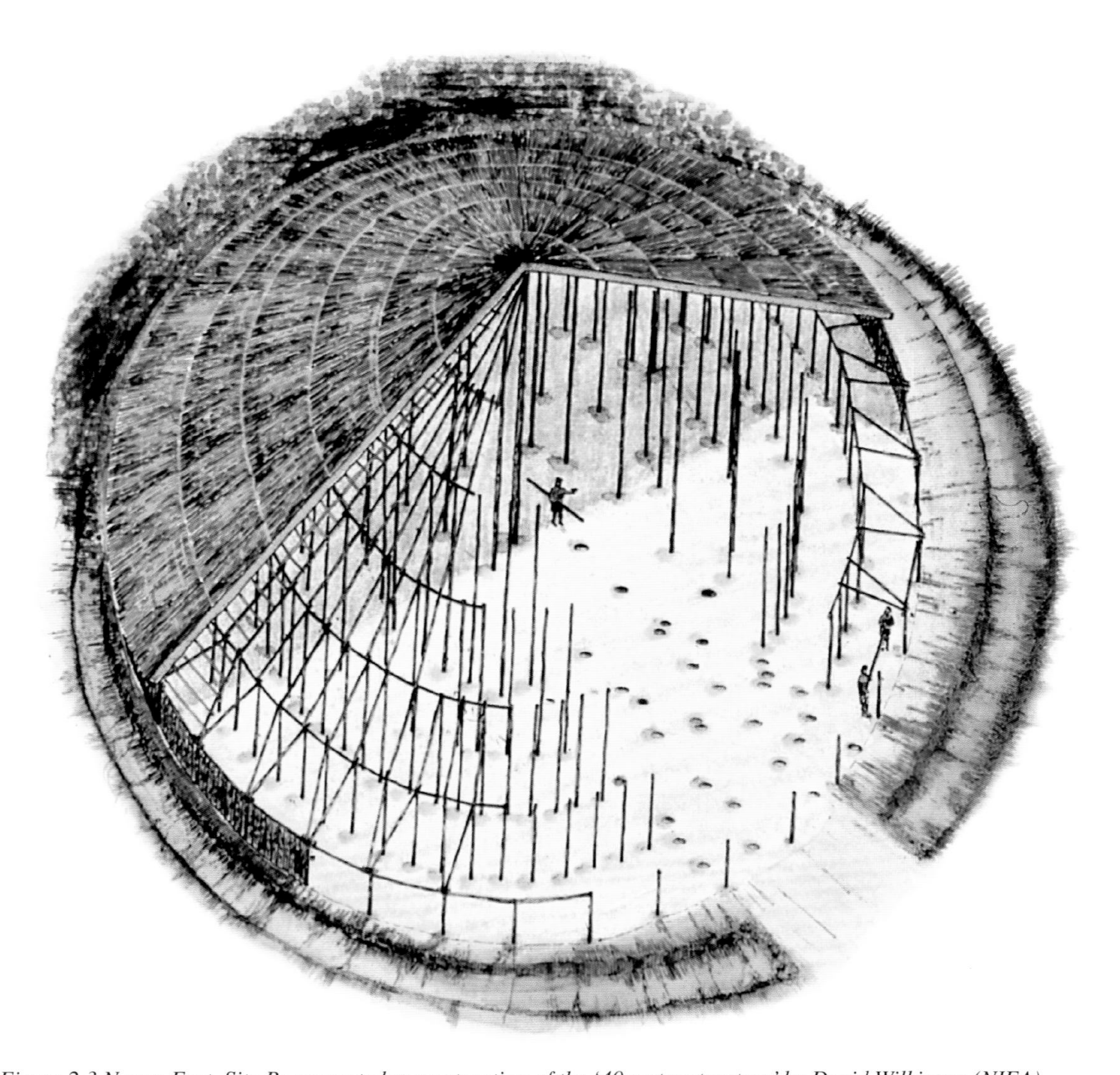

Figure 2.3 Navan Fort, Site B: suggested reconstruction of the '40 metre structure' by David Wilkinson (NIEA).

excavation in 1998 proved that this was also the date of construction of the surrounding ditched enclosure. A favoured, but by no means certain, interpretation is that the mound was constructed as a focus for assemblies or public ceremonies, perhaps to provide an appropriate outdoor setting for royal inauguration, the periodic proclamation of laws and the legitimisation of rulership. In this case we might imagine that it could have functioned like the Tynwald, a mound at St John's on the Isle of Man, which continues to be used down to the present day as an open-air 'parliament'. The Manx ruler, or his representative, sat on the top of the mound and his chief officials were arranged around on lower terraces according to their function, rank and number. The ordinary people gathered on the flat ground surrounding the mound to witness the proceedings on it, which closed with an acclamation. If, as seems possible, the mound in Navan Fort was built to be used for kingship ceremonies, it would have been an early example of public architecture. Even the gathering of the necessary quantities of timber, stones and earth and the labour needed in building and digging, made the construction of the mound and the earthwork enclosure a public event in itself.

Plate 2.6 Surface of the cairn found under the mound of turves at Site B (NIEA).

One of the major unanswered questions from the Navan excavations is the position of the original entrance to the large ditched enclosure encircling the hill. The embankment has been levelled over long stretches, destroying evidence for the original site of the entrance. On the balance of probabilities it should lie low down on the hill somewhere in the eastern perimeter. A procession approaching the site from this direction would pass Loughnashade, a lake immediately east of Navan, in which offerings were deposited in the Iron Age. This approach would have had the most gradual ascent of the hill and it would travel the longest distance within the sacred enclosure. The hilltop mound, the probable focus of any ceremony, would have been invisible, only slowly revealing itself against the western sky as the party moved up the slope.

The Site B mound was not the first structure built on the hilltop at Navan. Underneath there were several earlier phases of wooden structures, the designs of which remain puzzling. There were at least three successive examples of large figure-of-eight buildings pre-dating the construction of the large mound, all destroyed by fire, and with associated palisades or fences forming approach 'avenues' (Figure 2.4). In 1994 a geophysical survey found a 'new' figure-of-eight on the hilltop east of the mound; its smaller southern circular component was the 'house' found under the ring-barrow (Site A) in 1961.

So far, figure-of-eight structures have only been found in Iron Age sanctuaries in Ireland at Navan Fort and at Knockaulin, County Kildare and they can be said to be a characteristic of the public architecture of these sites. Their significance is emphasised by the discovery of two unusual finds, which even if found in isolation would be considered remarkable. The filling of one of the Navan wall trenches contained the well-preserved skull of a Barbary ape and one of the trenches of the figure-of-eight structures at Knockaulin produced an Iron Age sword.

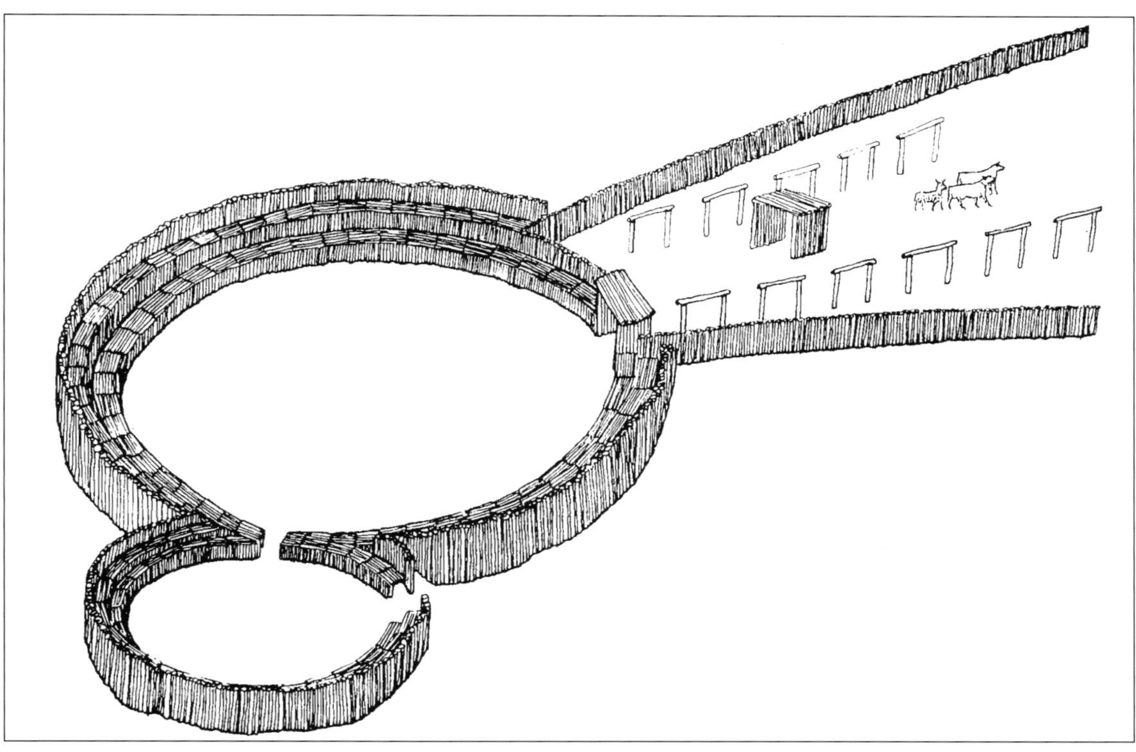

Figure 2.4 Reconstruction drawing, by Stephen Condon, of one of the Iron Age figure-of-eight structures found under the Site B mound at Navan Fort (NIEA).

At present we must admit to uncertainty as to the nature and construction method of the figure-of-eight buildings. With the rings ranging in diameter from 12m to over 30m it seems unlikely that they could have been roofed using methods normally envisaged for prehistoric houses. The southern elements had simple gap entrances on the east, but the northern components had wider gaps on the east, which were approached along fenced 'avenues'. The structures had burned down, probably set on fire deliberately, and do not appear to have been used for ordinary domestic occupation or for any other utilitarian purpose. Their unique design and presence in a major sanctuary of the Early Iron Age surely indicates that they were built and used for public ceremonial purposes.

We have little or no evidence for the design of dwellings in Iron Age Ireland. But the woven wicker-basket type houses, common in the Early Medieval period and known from AD 600 and later, are likely to represent the end of a long prehistoric tradition of circular house building, rather than the invention of a new type. If the houses of Iron Age Ireland were circular, defined by two rings of stakes and were sometimes joined to make a figure-of-eight plan, these might be important correspondences with the much larger ceremonial buildings of similar plan at the public sanctuaries. It could be suggested that the Iron Age figure-of-eight structures used for public ceremonies were large copies of contemporary houses. We could go even further and speculate that they might have been roofed using a robust, large-scale version of the basketry dome used on Early Medieval period houses. Anyone care to fund an experimental reconstruction?

Further reading

Waterman, D.M. 1997 *Excavations at Navan Fort 1961–71*, completed and edited by C.J. Lynn (Northern Ireland Archaeological Monographs: 3). Belfast: The Stationery Office.

The excavation and restoration of a seventeenth-century Irish formal garden: Lisburn Castle Gardens, County Antrim

Ruairí Ó Baoill and Stefanie McMullen

As part of a jointly-funded restoration project by the Heritage Lottery Fund and Lisburn City Council, two seasons of archaeological excavation were carried out at Lisburn Castle Gardens Park in 2003 and 2006, both by Archaeological Development Services Ltd. The excavations represent one of the most detailed investigations of a high status formal seventeenth-century garden in Ireland. The restoration and reconstruction of the gardens were largely based on the superb preservation of features and structures that the excavations revealed. The restored gardens were formally reopened in June 2008.

In 1611, James I granted to Sir Fulke Conway the Manor of Killultagh in the south-west of what is now modern County Antrim. It consisted of 50,000 acres and stretched from the Crumlin River in the north to Lough Neagh in the west and to the River Lagan in the south. His principal residence at Lisnagarvey (the old name of Lisburn) was at an important crossing point of the River Lagan and on the main route between Dublin and Carrickfergus. As stipulated in the 1611 grant, Conway built a manor house in a prominent position on top of a hill, commanding good views in all directions. The manor house or 'castle', which no longer survives above ground, was accompanied by a large formal garden the layout of which was initiated by Conway.

The seventeenth-century gardens, coterminous in extent with the modern Castle Gardens Park, can be divided into three distinct zones; the first of these is the area to the east and constitutes at least four curving terraces, now covered with grass and mature trees. The second area is to the south and consists of a walled enclosure divided into four linear terraces with supporting brick walls. The third area lies to the north of the terraced garden and occupies relatively flat ground, containing the seventeenth-century bowling green, together with the main part of the Victorian park lying beyond. Most of the archaeological investigations took place within the terraced garden and on the bowling green, though some works were carried out in the main area of the Victorian park. Surprisingly, given the site's prominent location, no features or artefacts dating to earlier than the seventeenth century were uncovered.

The first phase of garden use appears to date to the time of Sir Fulke Conway, most probably in the 1620s. A second phase of garden improvements began in the mid seventeenth century. This later work was overseen by George Rawdon, who had been appointed agent to the Conway estates in Ireland in 1631. Rawdon subsequently married into the Conway family and was resident at the Lisburn manor house from 1654. Letters from Rawdon to the Conway relatives in England, starting in 1656, describe the ongoing improvements he was undertaking at Lisburn, which included the employment of a Dutch gardener, work on the terraced gardens, filling in the fishpond, laying out paths, and various other building works.

Of the mid seventeenth-century works, the most visually imposing is the terraced garden constructed to the south of the manor house. Four linear terraces, separated by red brick walls, were erected within and enclosed by the walls. These replaced Conway's earlier curving terraces in this part of the gardens. Excavation showed that the original grass-banked terraces were revetted with the red brick walls and filled in to create the wider linear terraces. There may also have been a pond at the extreme south of the original garden uncovered during the excavations on the lowest terrace. This feature, if indeed it was a pond, was infilled by Rawdon and a red brick boundary wall built across it. The terraces, which became the focus of the mid and late seventeenth-century gardens, were criss-crossed with pathways of crushed brick and chalk, edged with flowerbeds, and perhaps also low hedging. Unfortunately there is little surviving documentation on the planting scheme of the gardens apart from a 1669 letter, from Rawdon to Lord Conway, in which reference is made to the gardens and to 'French seeds' and 'trees from Bordeaux'.

A calamitous fire took place in Lisburn in 1707 and it had a disastrous effect on the manor and its associated gardens. The manor was levelled and never rebuilt, and the gardens went into decline and neglect. How much damage the fire caused to the structures that stood within the garden is not fully known, but it may have been considerable. Dr Molyneux, who visited Lisburn in 1708 wrote: "... Lord Conway . . . his House, tho' at a distant from all the rest in the Town, burnt to Ashes, and all his Gardens in the same condition...".

Among Rawdon's other additions to the garden were a staircase perron, a turret and a gazebo, all located around the uppermost garden terrace and the adjacent bowling green, commanding fine views to the south of the river and the surrounding landscape. These were demolished after the fire of 1707, but were happily rediscovered during the recent excavations and subsequently restored.

The staircase perron, when first encountered in 2003, was completely overgrown and difficult to interpret, but subsequent excavation showed the surviving features to form part of a grand double staircase leading from the centre of the bowling green onto the terrace below. The perron walls were lined with red brick, and had a stone core, with sandstone slabs used for the steps or risers. A stone-built and vaulted shelter with sandstone quoins was incorporated into the perron superstructure. This may have been used as a grotto, a shaded area to rest, or perhaps to display a statue or specimen plant. After the fire of 1707 the perron was modified as an enclosed platform overlooking the area of the garden terraces, which is how it remained until the excavations uncovered its true splendour (Plates 2.7 and 2.8).

Plate 2.7 The overgrown perron at Lisburn Castle Gardens in 2003, pre-excavation (ADS Ltd).

Plate 2.8 The restored perron in 2009 (NIEA).

Artefacts found below the vaults of the staircase perron included fragments of highly decorated garden pots which depicted cherubs and motifs of fruit in relief. These may have originally been placed along the walls of the terraces to add visual interest to the garden. Fragments of glazed Dutch wall tiles, imported around 1667 by Rawdon, were also recovered. The tiles depict scenes with sea creatures, mermaids and winged cherubs (Plates 2.9, 2.10 and 2.11), and may have been used to decorate the walls.

Plates 2.9, 2.10 and 2.11 A selection of seventeenth-century tin-glazed Dutch wall tiles found during the excavation of the perron in 2006 (photographs reproduced courtesy of the Irish Linen Centre and Lisburn Museum).

The semicircular turret is located at the end of a long pathway in the eastern corner of the uppermost terrace of the walled garden, and south-east of the staircase perron. It is built of red brick with a stone and mortar base. The structure provided a vantage point over the gardens and might also have had a defensive function, though there is no evidence for this. The doorway was later blocked up and the interior filled in. Finds from the turret included fragments of seventeenth-century fine glassware and pottery sherds of high quality tableware and it is probable that these derived from the gazebo located uphill from it.

The gazebo was previously unknown prior to the excavations and is not portrayed in the mid seventeenth-century map of the town, *The Ground Plotte of Lisnegarvey* which depicts the manor house with its various outbuildings including a kitchen garden, stables and brewhouse. Such garden buildings were popular in the seventeenth century, though this is the first time one has been excavated in Ireland. It was located in the south-east corner of the bowling green on a higher level above the turret. It has been interpreted as a gazebo or summer house, built to take advantage of the fine views across the gardens and to be enjoyed by the manor house residents for socialising and dining. An entire basement room was found containing four ovens, which was accessed from the bowling green via steps (Plate 2.12). The upper level (or levels) of the building, where guests would have been served food and drink prepared below, has not survived. Excavation also uncovered fragments of the glass and pottery vessels used to store, cook and serve the food and drink. Other small finds included clay tobacco pipes, seventeenth-century coins and tokens, a circular carved bone gaming piece and a bronze pin brooch. The two tokens are of particular interest as they were separately stamped with the names of two individuals, one of whom, Edward Moore, was a gentleman who lived in Lisburn, and the date 1666.

During ground works in the northern part of the park in 2006 several areas of stone and mortar foundations were uncovered. These

Plate 2.12 The basement room of the gazebo, fully excavated in 2006. The brick-edged steps lead down from the bowling green and three ovens are visible in the opposite corner of the room (NIEA).

seem to correlate with the location of the manor house's outbuildings and enclosed gardens based on the seventeenth-century map. Their discovery strongly suggests that the foundations of the manor house and associated buildings, demolished after the fire in 1707, still survive below ground in the park. The manor house is portrayed on the Lisnegarvey map as roughly E-shaped in plan and it is possible that it may have resembled the manor house at Richhill, County Armagh, built in the 1660s.

After the fire, the manor house was demolished and the associated gardens were not re-established. Between the mid eighteenth century and the present day, Lisburn Castle Gardens were moulded into the form that is broadly familiar to visitors today. The area was transformed into a municipal garden for the town in the late Victorian period, when it was given among other things an avenue of mature trees, lawns, flower beds and a Wallace Drinking Fountain, the latter commemorating Richard Wallace (1818–1890) the park's owner and benefactor. In 1901 the park was bequeathed by his son to the town and although the northern area of the park was subsequently well cared for, the old garden brick terraces continued to be neglected. It is perhaps ironic, but fortuitous, that this neglect largely protected the remains of the seventeenth-century formal gardens until the restoration work and excavations commenced in 2003.

CHAPTER 3
Waterways

Chapter 3: Waterways

Introduction

Our familiarity with road and rail, and even air transport makes it difficult to appreciate the former significance of waterways. Until relatively recent times, waterborne transport of goods and people would have been the norm with the sea, navigable rivers and lakes, and latterly canals functioning as the main arteries of society and focus of settlement. The antiquity of the relationship between people and waterways is such that the oldest place-names in the landscape almost always include those of the major rivers. In Ptolemy's second-century AD gazetteer of the principal places and peoples of Ireland he references 6 promontories, 10 towns (*polis*), 16 tribes and 15 rivers, including the mouths of the rivers Logia, Argita and Vidva – possibly the Lagan, Bann and Foyle.

Given the intensive usage of waterways, the potential wealth of associated archaeology is high despite the difficulties of access such environments often present. The excavation undertaken on the small Dunnyneill Island in Strangford Lough (discussed in this chapter), for example, was run as a student training dig and presented a number of logistical difficulties. The excavation of the tide mill further north in the lough on Mahee Island at Nendrum (see Chapter 4) and the survey of the logboat in Greyabbey Bay (discussed in this chapter) on the opposite side of the lough, could both only be undertaken at low tides with the excavations being covered twice daily by the rising tide. The latter two sites were discovered during the intertidal survey of Strangford Lough conducted in the 1990s when a total of 606 sites such as fish traps, slipways, fords and a multitude of other features were catalogued and subsequently published in *Strangford Lough: an archaeological survey of the maritime cultural landscape*. As with the excavations, the survey was conducted at irregular hours to coincide with falling and low tides. The task of recording the *Taymouth Castle* shipwreck was no less arduous as it lies on the seabed under many metres of seawater (see below). Alternative methods of investigation also extend to the archaeology of the Rivers Bann and Blackwater where objects were recovered throughout the 1990s during dredging operations and with the aid of metal detectorists (see also in this chapter).

Waterways suggest movement; the movement of the water itself and the fish plants and animals it supports; the carriage of broken branches, leaves and lost goods in eddies downstream; and the movement of people in boats and rafts across the surface. The first settlers to Ireland and subsequent migrants, along with their belongings and (young) livestock, all had to come to Ireland by sea from various starting points. Early sea craft – skin boats, dug-out logboats and planked vessels – only rarely survive but their design and evolution, in the historic period at least, can be traced through early texts such as the legendary 'Voyage of St Brendan the Abbot' (*Navigatio sancti Brendani abbatis*), as well as through the occasional illustration. The Norse greatly influenced boat building in Ireland and introduced many nautical terms which are still in use in the Irish language, while the Anglo-Normans brought in further improvements in boat building. There have been two recent excavations of sea craft in the north of Ireland, both summarised in this chapter, though the pair could not be more different. One is a Neolithic logboat just 10m in length and around 5,000 years old, while the other is a complex composite structure over 50m in length and less than 150 years old. These boats represent just two examples of the wide variety of craft that once plied the coastal and inland waterways of Ireland.

As with the movement of people to and from Ireland, the movement and trade of goods would also have relied heavily on water transport as the cargo of the shipwrecked *Taymouth Castle* illustrates. English customs records and Ulster port books from the sixteenth and seventeenth centuries show that many numerous small boats shuttled between ports in the Irish Sea at that time ferrying cargos of fish, livestock, hides, linen and wool (exports) as well as wine, coal, iron and salt (imports). There were fluctuations in the goods bought and sold depending on duties, stocking levels and wars and there was also the very real danger of piracy and shipwreck. The majority of sites discussed in this volume have produced imported goods that would have travelled by sea to get here – the Limoges figure on the Drumadoon bell shrine (see Chapter 1), German stoneware found at Castle Hill, Dungannon (see Chapter 5) and at Movanagher (see Chapter 1), a Continental bowl recovered from the River Blackwater (see below in this chapter), and most remarkably, a Barbary ape skull found at Navan Fort (see Chapter 2)!

Access to water, in particular rivers and ports, also influenced the distribution of the emerging industries of the eighteenth and nineteenth centuries. Navigable waterways were required to import the vast quantities of fuel and raw materials that they needed (see Ballymacarett glassworks, Chapter 4) while rivers were harnessed to power the waterwheels of the numerous mills at the heart of these new industrial ventures. Almost a millennium earlier, the monks on Mahee Island engineered a mill to harness the waterpower of the twice daily rise of the tide (see discussion of Nendrum in Chapter 4) an energy resource only now being given serious reconsideration.

The importance of waterways is not limited to the functional qualities of transport, trade and water power. Bodies of water also function as readymade boundaries – the River Lagan for example demarcates part of the boundary between Counties Antrim and Down. Waterways have also often been imbued with symbolism, in particular in late prehistory. The majority of provenanced Irish Bronze Age swords have been recovered from 'watery places' such as bogs, lakes and rivers indicating ritual practices and probable votive depositions. The transition between the Late Bronze Age and Early Iron Age coincides with an environmental downturn and it has been suggested that the votive deposition of objects in watery places and ritual pools at this time may have been carried out in an attempt to appease the gods. Perhaps the most impressive of these is the little gold boat found as part of an Early Iron Age hoard at Broighter, near the River Roe, in the late nineteenth century. The small lake of Loughnashade located adjacent to Navan Fort (see Chapter 2) yielded a human skull, and four large bronze horns and these have also all been interpreted as offerings to gods.

The theme of 'Waterways' is therefore broad and in many ways can be extended to incorporate most of the sites included in this book reflecting its importance in all aspects of life.

Strangford's oldest shipwreck: a Neolithic logboat from Greyabbey Bay, County Down

Wes Forsythe

Visitors to the Greyabbey Bay area of Strangford Lough cannot fail to be impressed by the large expanse of sandy seabed uncovered at low tide. This affords the opportunity for long walks, collecting shellfish and bait, or simply enjoying the wide vistas to Scrabo Hill and the surrounding shores. For the archaeologist this part of Strangford's shores is especially fascinating, for as the tide recedes an archaeological landscape emerges that is virtually unparalleled in richness on any other stretch of the Irish coastline. The range of monuments on this foreshore reflects the long story of coastal changes and man's interaction with the sea. These include the remains of an ancient forest, which was drowned by rising sea levels 9,000 years ago, and remnants of wooden and stone fishtraps, which were in operation throughout the Medieval period. The remains of a boat carved from a single oak log, abandoned some 5,000 years ago, have also been located on the Greyabbey foreshore.

Logboats are the most common type of ancient boats found in Ireland, although they have been in use for a long time, dating from as early as the Mesolithic period and recorded in historical sources up to the eighteenth century. It is known that skin boats, the ancestors of the currachs and coracles, were also in use since at least the Iron Age, but these lightweight vessels are much rarer in the archaeological record. Boats have naturally been a feature of life in Ireland since the island was first inhabited. The first people to colonise the island had to arrive by sea, putting boats amongst the earliest items that prehistoric Irish people had at their disposal. Boats were widely used on the many rivers and inland loughs that acted as the main communication routes through the country, and the majority of logboat finds of all ages come from these bodies of water. This is one of the reasons why the Greyabbey Bay logboat is of particular significance – it is one of only a few logboats discovered in a maritime environment. Maritime logboats have also been discovered in Larne Lough, County Antrim, Cahore, County Wexford and at Gormanstown, County Meath. Other logboats from the Strangford Lough area have been found in the Quoile River, notably from Inch where a ferry was known to operate since at least the sixteenth century. Of these examples, one has been dated to the Late Neolithic/Early Bronze Age, while another produced a date placing it in the Early Medieval period. The survival of these maritime logboats can be attributed to a low-energy marine environment on the less exposed eastern coast and the soft sediment they came to rest in.

The Greyabbey Bay logboat was discovered in the winter of 2000 partially exposed on the intertidal flats at low water. A short excavation was undertaken to completely expose and record the vessel on the shore and a small trench was excavated under it to obtain the profile of the hull (Plate 3.1). One end of the logboat had come to rest slightly higher than the other and this resulted in it, the south-eastern part, being more eroded than the rest of the boat, which being buried managed to preserve some features including the height of the gunwales. The exterior and interior hull was generally smooth and featureless, with the exception of the north-west end. A rounded, internal bevel at this end provided a wide, flat tip to the boat. Below this on the floor there was a low, transverse ridge. This ridge would have given the rower's feet some purchase as the vessel was underway.

During the excavation the loose sand and shellfish were cleared from around the vessel which showed that the boat was lying in sticky mud underlain with compact sand. Finds from the northern underside of the vessel include worked fragments of wattle rods, which came from the decaying Medieval fishtraps upstream and demonstrate that the boat has been periodically exposed and reburied over the centuries by moving sediment. There were no obvious signs of motive for its abandonment, or evidence for a swift sinking – a small leakage toward the north-west end was present but this was due to wood-boring organisms weakening the hull at this point, rather than a fatal puncture. After the boat was recorded it was reburied (Plate 3.2). The soft-sediment, low-energy environment of the site has preserved it for millennia and will continue to do so as long as the boat is not exposed.

During the excavation a small sample of the wood was taken for radiocarbon dating and this returned a date range of 3499–3032 BC placing it in the Neolithic. The Neolithic is associated with the introduction of agriculture including the cultivation of crops and farming of domestic animals. In this context the logboat from Greyabbey Bay could have been used to move people, their farming produce and animals around the calm waters of the lough, as well as for fishing trips or to collect shellfish. Megalithic tombs on the shores of the lough, as well as a number of finds of pottery, axes and arrowheads attest to the presence of a Neolithic community in the area, most notably on the western and southern shores. The Greyabbey Bay logboat by contrast stands as one of the few Neolithic finds from the Ards side of the lough.

Plate 3.1 Recording the Greyabbey Bay logboat with the Ards Peninsula in the distance (NIEA).

Plate 3.2 The reburied site – the Greyabbey Bay logboat after conservation (W. Forsythe).

The archaeological monuments on the Greyabbey foreshore have been scheduled. They are therefore protected by legislation in recognition of the outstanding maritime cultural landscape in the bay and this protection includes the rare maritime logboat.

Further reading

Forsythe, W. and Gregory, N. 2007 'A Neolithic logboat from Greyabbey Bay, Co. Down', *Ulster Journal of Archaeology* 66, 6–13.

Beauties of the Bann and Blackwater: reflections on riverine archaeology in Northern Ireland

Cormac Bourke

Sir William Wilde was among the first to appreciate the importance of rivers in Irish archaeology. His three-volume catalogue of the collections of the Royal Irish Academy, published between 1857 and 1862, was inspired in part by the discovery of archaeological material in Ireland's rivers during drainage in the mid nineteenth century.

Wilde refers to hundreds of Neolithic stone axes, dozens of Bronze Age tools and weapons and numerous Medieval pins and brooches. But despite this rich harvest, riverine archaeology was slow to develop. Later drainage was monitored piecemeal, if at all, and many opportunities for archaeological discovery were lost in the twentieth century. Drainage of the Bann in the 1930s yielded hundreds of artefacts, including a decorated bronze disc of Iron Age date (the 'Bann disc',

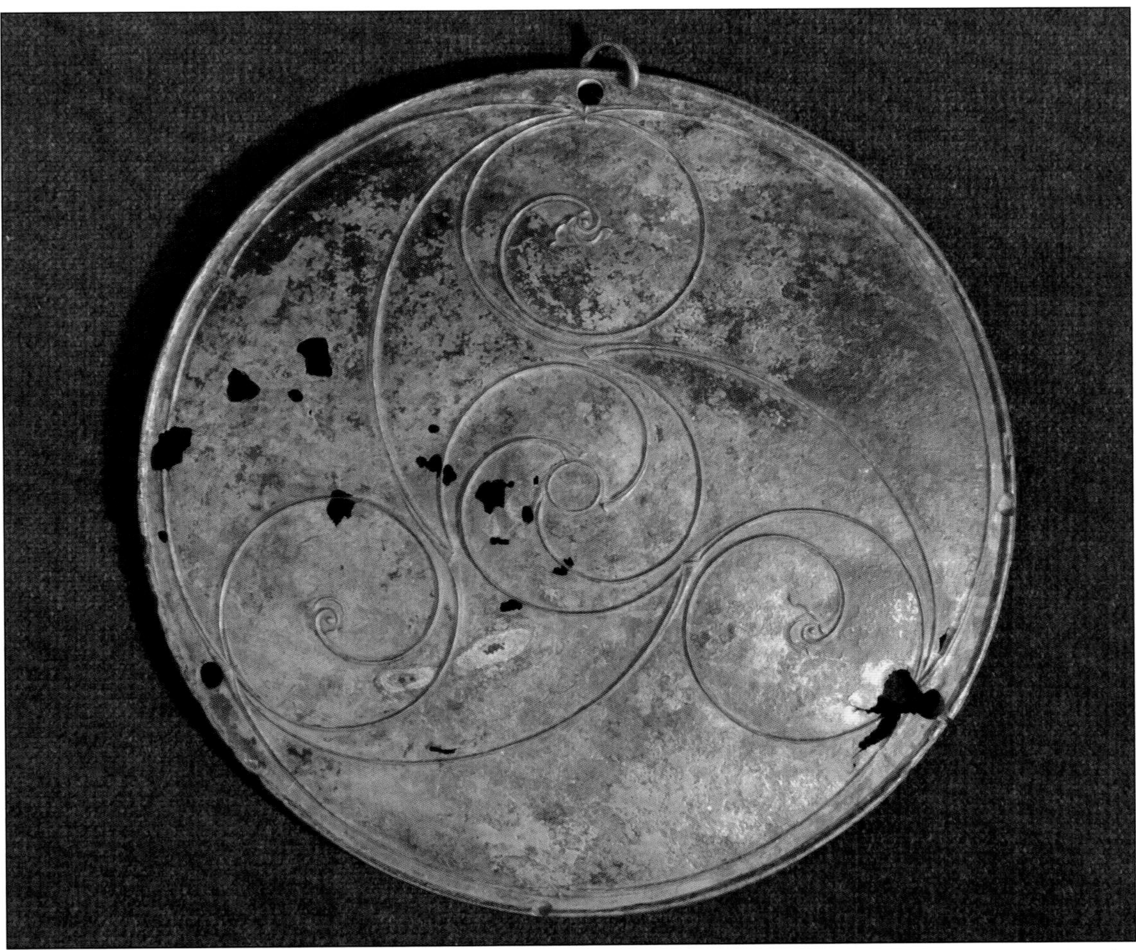

Plate 3.3 The Bann disc, recovered from the River Bann at Loughan Island near Coleraine (photograph reproduced courtesy of the Trustees of National Museums Northern Ireland).

for long the logo of the Ulster Museum – Plate 3.3) and the only complete Medieval crozier extant today in Northern Ireland, but recovery was patchy and there was no consistent archaeological supervision. More recently, in the 1990s, the Ulster Museum was involved in the systematic recovery of material subsequent to the drainage of the River Blackwater in Counties Armagh and Tyrone. This was the first exercise of its kind in Irish archaeology and involved working with local metal detectorists who made the initial discoveries.

The discovery of artefacts in Irish rivers is not new; witness the record in the *Annals of the Four Masters* for 1178: "The [River Corrib] was dried up for a period of a ... day; all the articles that had been lost in it from remotest times ... were collected by ... the people of the country". The Four Masters clearly refer to the finding of what we would call archaeological material, but many other finds must have escaped written record.

How did valuable material come to be in rivers in the first place? There are, conventionally, two explanations: accidental loss and ritual deposition. The latter, it seems, can account for Bronze Age and Iron Age finds in lakes and bogs. But we lack clear evidence for ritual deposition in rivers, and there were any number of circumstances in which accidental losses might have occurred. There is an early reference to loss in a river in the eighth-century *Táin Bó Cuailnge:* "Then Cú Chulainn cast the javelin after him and it lighted on the hollow at the back of his head ... And the bronze from the spear landed on the stream".

This brings together a confrontation at a ford and the loss of a weapon and is doubtless a literary reflection of a commonplace reality. Fords were crucial in negotiating river crossings and were habitually used until recent times. The element *áth* ('ford') is widespread in Irish place-names, as in Athlone (*Áth Luain*), Aughnacloy (*Áth na Cloiche*), Annalong (*Áth na Long*) and many more. Clearly there is a correlation between fords and concentrations of archaeological finds. But we must suspend our impression of a river as necessarily a water-course of one channel; it is possible (topography permitting) that rivers divided into multiple shallow channels which were periodically blocked by fallen trees. The traveller facing the obstacle of a river might have crossed several channels by a series of more or less reliable fords.

The archaeology of bridges is only now receiving attention. Parts of a timber bridge were discovered in the 1990s in the Shannon at Clonmacnoise and date to around AD 804. A record of 1120 mentions two bridges on the same river built under royal direction, both of them sited at pre-existing fords, and it seems that bridge-building was something of a royal prerogative. An east-Ulster king who died in 789 was known as Fiachna Dub Droichtech, 'dark Fiachna the bridge-builder', and we read in a saga of Brian Boru that "by him were made bridges and causeways and highroads". Wood was the raw material in most cases; for in 1360 the *Annals of the Four Masters* record, as though it were unusual, the building of a "bridge of lime and stone" at Ballysadare. The instigator, unsurprisingly, was a king.

The probability that rivers were generally shallower and slower flowing than they are today implies that they froze more easily. The annals mention freezing conditions and passage on the ice of frozen rivers and lakes. For 817 the *Annals of Ulster* record:

> "There was abnormal ice and much snow from the Epiphany to Shrovetide. The Boyne and other rivers were crossed dry-footed; lakes likewise. Herds and hunting parties were on Lough Neagh, and wild deer were hunted. The materials for a wooden church were ... brought ... from the lands of Connacht over Upper and Lower Lough Erne."

People attempting to cross ice no doubt sometimes misjudged the conditions and met with misadventure. Such accidents perhaps explain the discovery of artefacts in rivers and lakes in some cases.

Boating accidents happened as well, and the discovery over the years of hundreds of logboats is evidence that rivers were significant channels of communication. The earliest such craft have been dated to the Neolithic period in Ireland and their life extended until at least the seventeenth century AD (as discussed in more detail by Wes Forsythe in this chapter). According to the *Annals of Ulster*, the abbot of Armagh met with misadventure, perhaps when travelling by boat, in 1118: "The value of one hundred ounces of the mass-equipment of Cellach, successor of Patrick, was drowned in the Dabhall [the Blackwater], and he himself received a shock." Here is one way in which ecclesiastical metalwork might have come to rest on the bed of the River Blackwater. And although that river has yielded material of all periods from the Mesolithic to the present day, its Medieval metalwork will claim our attention here.

Pride of place is taken by the Clonmore shrine (Plates 3.4 and 3.5). So called from its discovery at Clonmore in north County Armagh, the shrine was found in spoil which had been dredged from the Blackwater around 1970. The first pieces came to light in 1990 and further parts were found in

Plate 3.4 The Clonmore shrine from Clonmore, County Armagh: front view (photograph reproduced courtesy of the Trustees of National Museums Northern Ireland).

Plate 3.5 The Clonmore shrine: back view (photograph reproduced courtesy of the Trustees of National Museums Northern Ireland).

Plate 3.6 Enamelled mounts from Shanmullagh, County Armagh (photograph reproduced courtesy of the Trustees of National Museums Northern Ireland).

1991, 2000 and 2001. Made of tinned bronze plates, the shrine dates from the late seventh century and housed relics of a Christian saint or saints. It is decorated in native, 'late Celtic' style but is Classical in form and represents a tomb in miniature. And miniature is the word, for the shrine is only 82mm long, 80mm high and 27mm deep. It was designed to be carried on a strap around the neck, rendering the power of relics portable while sheltering its precious source. The Clonmore shrine is the earliest known piece of Christian metalwork from Ireland and illustrates the marriage of pre-Christian art with a Classical, Christian form.

Some 7km upstream from Clonmore, on opposite sides of the river, lie the townlands of Derryoghil, County Tyrone, and Shanmullagh, County Armagh. Here, perhaps at an ancient ford, the stock-in-trade of a metalworker was lost in the years around 900. He was dealing in both Irish and Viking-influenced (or 'Hiberno-Viking') metalwork and was himself perhaps of mixed ancestry. He had access – by whatever means – to a church treasury (probably that of Armagh), and was carrying ecclesiastical metalwork destined for recycling, as well as a complete bronze wine-strainer and a hanging-bowl. Silver bracelets and a gold finger-ring are in Hiberno-Viking style (Plate v), as are lead weights set with fragments of ecclesiastical metalwork (Plate 3.6); similar weights have been found at Kilmainham/Islandbridge in the ninth-century cemetery of the Dublin Vikings.

The Shanmullagh hoard is unique in Irish archaeology and includes types of objects more typically found in Norwegian Viking graves. Our metalworker was part of the chain of supply which catered for the international markets of the Viking age.

While the hanging-bowl in the Shanmullagh hoard was made in Ireland in the ninth century, another bowl from the Blackwater, at Corr and Dunavally, above Charlemont, County Armagh, was made on the Continent in the twelfth century and imported to Ireland soon afterwards (Plate A.1). Such vessels were used for hand-washing in churches, religious communities and wealthy households and were widely traded across Europe. The inner surface of the Blackwater example bears engraved figures of personified Virtues and its closest counterpart comes from the Danube in Vienna. What makes the bowl exceptional is that it was adapted for suspension by an Irish metalworker who added mounts and hooks below the rim, something its original maker never intended. The effect was to modify a Continental vessel in conformity with Irish taste, indicating the tenacity of the native tradition of the hanging-bowl.

Mention must be made, finally, of a series of Late Medieval swords. At least eight such swords are now known from the Blackwater, including an old find in the National Museum of Ireland. Three (in the Ulster Museum) are especially noteworthy: one, made in northern England or Scandinavia, is a rare type with lobate pommel and downturned guard (Plate 3.7); another, with inlaid decoration and a lustrous black coating, is of Polish or German origin; another – an Irish ring-pommel sword of a well-known type – is exceptional in the length and quality of its blade.

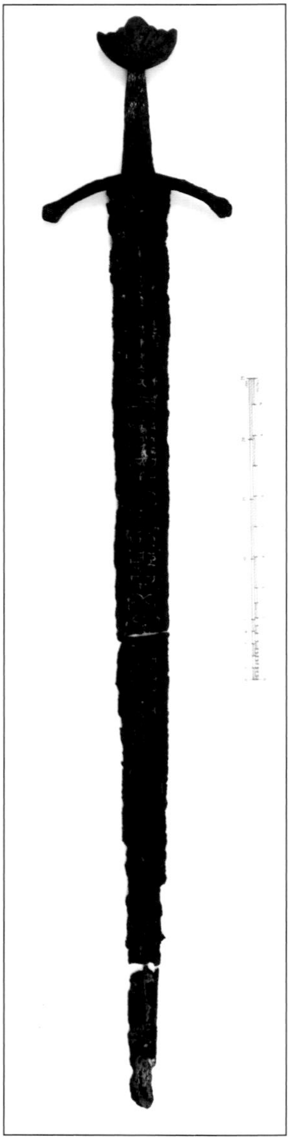

Plate 3.7 Iron sword from Maghery, County Armagh (photograph reproduced courtesy of the Trustees of National Museums Northern Ireland).

All of this is but a flavour of the archaeology of rivers in general and of the Blackwater in particular, and of the riches accruing to the Ulster Museum through a systematic programme of acquisition and recovery in the field. The same strategy, given support and resources, might be repeated with similar results elsewhere.

Further reading

Bourke, C. 1993 'Antiquities from the River Blackwater II, Iron Age metalwork', *Ulster Journal of Archaeology* 56, 109–13.

Bourke, C. 2001 'Antiquities from the River Blackwater III, iron axe-heads', *Ulster Journal of Archaeology* 60, 63–93.

Ramsey, G., Bourke, C. and Crone, D. 1991–92 'Antiquities from the River Blackwater I, Bronze Age metalwork', *Ulster Journal of Archaeology* 54–55, 138–49.

Dunnyneill Island: an Early Medieval emporium in Strangford Lough

Finbar McCormick and Philip Macdonald

The Dunnyneill Islands (Plate 3.8) comprise two adjacent islands located towards the southern end of Strangford Lough. The islands are linked by a causeway at low tide. The easternmost island and the causeway are both depositional features made up of shingle eroded from the adjacent island. The westernmost, and larger island, which is known as Dunnyneill Island, is a tree-covered drumlin that rises to a height of approximately 16m above the surrounding waters. It is one of the most striking islands in Strangford Lough because it rises so steeply from the water (Plate 3.9). Its profile is further exaggerated by the ongoing erosion on the island's southern face which has led to the formation of a steep cliff.

Plate 3.8 A view of the Dunnyneill Islands from the air (NIEA).

Plate 3.9 The western larger island, Dunnyneill Island, at low tide showing its raised elevation and eroded southern face (CAF).

Dunnyneill Island overlooks both the mouth of the Quoile Estuary and the entrance of the narrows into Strangford Lough. This location forms an optimal position to observe, and intercept, any maritime traffic entering the lough. Unusually for a drumlin, the summit of the island is flat. This flat plateau is surrounded by an irregular enclosure defined by a ditch and an inner and outer bank, and enclosing an area approximately 30m in diameter. The enclosure is augmented by a smaller annex of approximately $70m^2$, which is defined by a ditch and located on a slightly lower terrace. In addition to the enclosure and annex at the top of the island, traces of a low bank, which once apparently enclosed the base of the drumlin just above the high-tide line, survive on the western side of the island.

The continuing threat to the site posed by coastal erosion prompted the NIEA to fund the authors' excavations on the island during 2002 and 2003. Trenches were excavated within the interior of the main enclosure, across its banks and ditch, across the ditch separating the main enclosure and its annex, and across the earthwork at the base of the island. A wide range of finds, dating from the prehistoric period to the modern day, was recovered, and evidence for four phases of activity was identified. Interpreting activity on the island poses a challenge. Given the small size of Dunnyneill Island and its apparent lack of a permanent water supply, it is not obvious that a settlement could be either self-supporting or sustainable in the long term, suggesting that occupation would always have had a specialised and temporary or episodic character.

The earliest phase of activity was associated with the remains of a small hut (external diameter approximately 8m) with the outline of a wall marked by a single course of stones with a north-west-facing entrance). Radiocarbon dating suggests this hut was built some time after the middle of the seventh century AD. Artefacts recovered during the course of the excavation, which are of this date, include rare examples of imported pottery and vessel glass. The pottery is of a type (known as E-Ware) which was imported into Ireland from northern or western France during the late sixth and seventh centuries AD as part of a long-distance trade associated with luxury goods. The assemblage of vessel glass is large and mostly contains fragments of vessels of probable Anglo-Saxon origin of seventh or eighth century AD date, but also includes two sherds of Mediterranean origin of fifth or sixth century AD date. Finds of imported pottery and glass are rare in Ireland and sites on which they occur are usually interpreted as either high status settlements or trading centres known as emporia. E-Ware has previously been recovered from several sites in Strangford Lough and its coastal hinterland. This area has the densest distribution of E-Ware sites in Ireland, suggesting that it was probably an entry point for imported material into north-east Ireland. Both Downpatrick and Kilclief have previously been identified as possible points of entry for this material, however, the possibility that Dunnyneill Island may have formed the primary centre for the distribution of imported goods into the territory of the Dál Fiatach, with its principal royal centre located conveniently close by at Downpatrick, cannot be easily dismissed. Although there are no well defined landing places on the island, it is possible to land on the northern shore with relative ease. Given its strategic location it is probable that Dunnyneill Island functioned as an emporium during the Early Medieval period.

After the end of the seventh century, construction of the main enclosure's earthworks took place. This second phase of activity was associated with the construction of a long, sub-rectangular structure within the enclosure's interior which was represented archaeologically by a slab-lined feature – possibly the remains of a palisade or building. Animal bone from the fill of this feature had a radiocarbon date range from the eighth to tenth centuries, and dates derived from the primary fills of the enclosure's ditches suggest that they had not begun to silt up until at least the eighth or ninth centuries. This evidence suggests that the site's second phase might be contemporary with the beginning of the Viking period in the ninth century. Annalistic references indicate that there were Viking settlements in Strangford Lough during this time, although whether the site's occupants were Vikings or native Irish is impossible to assess. Artefacts recovered from this second phase of activity demonstrated that a wide range of craft activities were being undertaken on the island, including metalworking and the assaying of silver. The animal bone assemblage recovered from the first two phases of activity resembles that from known contemporary high status sites, and contains a relatively high proportion of quality beef, which was presumably supplied from the mainland.

The features and deposits associated with the Early Medieval phases of occupation were sealed by a featureless soil horizon. A spread of articulated animal bones recovered from this layer provided a radiocarbon date of eighth or ninth century AD. Datable finds from the soil included a copper-alloy stud-headed stick pin dated from the mid eleventh to early thirteenth century AD and sherds of a locally produced type of pottery known as Souterrain Ware, several of which are decorated with cordons. Close dating of this pottery is difficult; however, it is unlikely that the cordoned forms pre-date the ninth century AD. It is probable that this third phase of activity represents a sustained period of non-intensive exploitation of Dunnyneill Island which lasted for an uncertain, but potentially extended, duration.

The archaeological evidence relating to the final phase is restricted to deposits associated with the deliberate demolition of the inner bank into the interior of the main enclosure and the deposition of levelling deposits, partially made up of beach gravels. Little of the bank material was incorporated into the ditch suggesting that the principal motivation in destroying the bank was not to remove the enclosure's boundary, but to create a flat plateau at the top of the island in order to facilitate a new phase of activity. The only recorded features associated with this phase were two spreads of flagstones laid out over the levelling deposits, which may either be the remains of a floor or footings for the walls of a building. No other structural evidence dating to this final phase was identified, probably because subsequent grazing of animals on the island resulted in the trampling of the ground surface and the truncation of any such evidence. Ironically, it was the destruction of the inner bank which led to the preservation of the archaeological remains associated with the earlier phases of activity. The overlying spread of rubble from the razed inner bank protected the deposits and features from being destroyed by the trampling of cattle that grazed on the island in the nineteenth century.

A precise date for this final phase of activity is uncertain; however, the stick pin noted above, which was recovered from the soil sealed by the inner bank's rubble, indicates that the levelling could not have occurred before the mid eleventh century. Given the lack of evidence for structures relating to this last phase of occupation it is difficult to assess either its character or duration. However, a copper-alloy buckle of late twelfth- to late fourteenth-century date, was recovered from the topsoil suggesting occupation extended into the Anglo-Norman period (Plate 3.10). This is around the time of John de Courcy's invasion of the north of Ireland in 1177. Given the strategic position of Dunnyneill Island, it may have been reoccupied during this period of political change and instability, although it is not possible to confidently identify the single historical episode which prompted the island's reoccupation. However, during the early thirteenth century de Courcy was expelled from Ulster and, according to the *Chronicle of the Kings of Mann and the Isles*, was forced to call upon the aid of the Manx fleet which landed at Strangford in 1205 in a failed attempt to regain his lands. It may have been this event, or possibly even its anticipation, which prompted the island's reoccupation.

Plate 3.10 A copper-alloy buckle of late twelfth- to late fourteenth-century date, recovered from the topsoil on Dunnyneill Island (CAF).

Further reading

McCormick, F. and Macdonald P. 2004 'Excavations at Dunnyneill Island, Strangford Lough', *Lecale Review* 2, 5–10.

The shipwreck *Taymouth Castle*

Colin Breen, Claire Callaghan-Breen and Máire Ní Loingsigh

On January 5th 1867 the *Taymouth Castle* was lost in severe weather off the Antrim coast. The wreck was discovered by sport divers more than a century later and the site was brought to the attention of archaeologists at Queen's University Belfast by a local diving club in 1995. The wreck site lies between Tornamoney Point and Runabay Point, off the east Antrim coast. The remains lie approximately 70m from the base of the cliffs, just beyond basal boulder collapse, in 15m of water. As a consequence of the serious damage being caused to the wreck by divers searching for souvenirs, the NIEA funded a detailed survey and limited excavation of the site in 1995.

The *Taymouth Castle* was built by the Connell Company of Glasgow, Scotland and was first launched on July 8th 1865. Lloyd's Register shows that the vessel weighed 627 tons and measured 172 ft (52.4m) in length, 29 ft (8.8m) in beam and 18 ft (5.5m) in depth. It was fully rigged and composite built, with iron framing and wooden planking. This was still a relatively new technique of shipbuilding at the time, as shipbuilders tried to combine the benefits of both materials. The *Taymouth Castle* was only on its second voyage when it was lost off the Irish coast en route from Broomielaw, the harbour of Glasgow, to Singapore carrying a mixed cargo valued at £50,000 and comprising ceramics, alcohol, cotton yarn and building materials.

Little of the original structure survives on the seabed due to its violent wrecking in 1867 and subsequent periods of prolonged storm damage. Two primary areas were investigated on the wreck site in 1995 (Plate 3.11). The first was an excavation trench opened up directly north of the surviving remains of part of the forward hull represented by a 7m-wide section of iron framing. A large windlass is attached to the western portion of this section and consists of a cylindrical iron drum with some wooden components, while the remains of its rotary gear are also visible. This would have been operated by inserting bars to manually turn the windlass to raise and lower the anchor. A series of iron links, presumably from an anchor chain, are concreted to the windlass. The chain continues off the iron framing into the sand on the starboard side, suggesting that the anchor had been dropped at the time of wrecking, but did not have the desired holding effect. A number of large copper-sheathed timbers, with copper-alloy bolts, lay exposed 35m to the north of the main area of wreckage which originally formed the outer planking of the hull.

Plate 3.11 The Taymouth Castle under excavation (CMA).

A second area of investigation took place on a mound formed by the concretion of numerous clusters of iron bowls stacked one inside the other with straw packing in between. The bowls were found to be British-made woks, although their precise place of origin is unknown. These bowls had corroded over time and concreted together to form a protective shell overlying a mass of pottery and bottles. Fragments of timber from a packing case, which would originally have contained the pottery and bottles, were discovered at the base of this mound.

The majority of the artefacts recovered from the site consisted of ceramics. Two distinct types were identified; Glaswegian spongeware, and blue and white transfer-printed ware and most of these pieces appear to have come from Bell's Pottery in Glasgow. The pottery was established early in the nineteenth century by John and Matthew Perston Bell and was one of the most successful potteries in Scotland. Much of Bell's products were exported to the Far East and at the height of its production era it provided employment to around 800 people. Spongeware was one of the first types of mass produced pottery, with large amounts destined for the export market. The process is thought to have originated in Scotland in the 1830s and then spread abroad. The term 'spongeware' derives from the decoration of the earthenware with a pattern created by dipping a cut sponge in coloured slip and applying the pattern to the partially fired 'biscuit-ware' before the final firing. The patterns were repeated on different pieces in various colours and were often

Plates 3.12 and 3.13 Examples of the colourful spongeware, made by Bell's Pottery in Glasgow, recovered from the Taymouth Castle (NIEA).

combined with hand-painted decoration, as is the case with the majority of the pottery from the *Taymouth Castle*. The collection from the site consisted of large rice bowls, dinner plates, soup dishes, small deep bowls, small conical bowls and saucers. The patterns varied greatly but were primarily floral. A range of approximately nine colours was used in the sponge-printed and hand-printed decoration, varying in clarity according to the strength of application and the effects of weathering, but the main colours were cornflower blue, violet blue, citrus green, grape purple, mulberry and yellow (Plates 3.12 and 3.13).

Other forms of pottery recovered included transfer-printed earthenware, a type of decorated ceramic thought to have been developed between 1720 and 1760. Pieces were decorated by transferring a design, engraved on copper plates, onto tissue paper. The printed side of the tissue was then placed on biscuit-ware before glazing, while the ink was still wet, until the ink was absorbed. The pottery was then rinsed in water to remove the tissue. Examples recovered from the wreck site include the well-known 'Bosphorus' pattern and the 'Wild Rose' pattern. The 'Bosphorus' pattern (Plate 3.14) was light blue and varied in quality, and soup dishes and dinner plates formed the greatest part of the collection. The 'Wild Rose' pattern was in dark blue and depicted an English rural scene along a river bank.

Two main types of bottles were found – glass and stoneware (Plate 3.15). A number of intact examples of both were discovered to still contain liquid substances which, on laboratory analysis were found to have an alcohol content of 7%. The type of alcoholic substance contained could not be identified but brandy, white wine, spirits, and beer were all listed in the cargo inventory. The glass bottles recovered from the *Taymouth Castle* were dark green in colour and seven intact ones were found during the excavation. Most of these were inscribed and the company names indicated that they originated in Edinburgh. Five examples even had the corks still in place, while other bottlenecks also had the wire that held the cork in place, still attached. Two examples had a wax and tinfoil seal over the cork and wire, one of which had the name 'Allsopp's India Pale Ale' imprinted on it. India Pale Ale commenced exportation during the 1790s while Allsopp's Pale Ale was first produced in 1822. This new type of ale was developed to overcome the difficulties with spoilage over the long journey to India. The new recipe involved more hops and higher alcohol content and also produced a lighter, more refreshing drink, appreciated in the Indian heat. It appears that the ale was originally transported in wooden casks and then transferred to bottles once it arrived at its destination. Eventually it was discovered that beer could be bottled prior to

Plate 3.14 One of the transfer-printed 'Bosphorus' pattern plates recovered from the Taymouth Castle (NIEA).

Plate 3.15 A selection of complete glass and stoneware bottles, with corks still in place, from the ship's cargo (NIEA).

transportation provided it had been left in barrels for 8 to 12 months first, otherwise the corks tended to pop out of the bottles.

Other artefactual evidence recovered included circular wooden deadeyes used as part of the ship's rigging system, a section of cloth-sheathed rope, leather fragments from saddles and bricks inscribed with 'Allan & Mann, Covan Patent, Glasgow'.

This excavation was the first licensed underwater shipwreck excavation in Northern Ireland. It was successful in recovering a body of information from an underwater site under serious threat from natural and cultural processes of destruction and has provided a unique insight into mid nineteenth-century marine trade and technology.

CHAPTER 4
Technology and Industry

Chapter 4: Technology and Industry

Introduction

Archaeologists have traditionally subdivided the past into phases, or 'Ages', based primarily on technological innovation. The dates assigned to these periods mark the first evidence for the use of a new material; they do not mark the end of older technologies which can, and typically do continue in use throughout succeeding decades, centuries and even millennia. The recovery of thousands of flint tools from Corrstown (see Chapter 1) and other contemporary sites, demonstrates that stone tool technology was still widely employed throughout the Bronze Age while the work of bronzesmiths rather than blacksmiths dominated the metallurgy of the Irish Iron Age. Mapping and dating the use of these technologies, indicate the rate and extent to which new innovations spread and were adopted.

The advent of the Neolithic and agriculture around 4000 BC introduced a whole new way of life and with it, associated new goods, technologies and tools. The most significant and ubiquitous of these in the archaeological record is pottery. It is probable that pots were initially made in all households but that over time specialist potters emerged along with an increasing range of decoration styles and forms. In terms of stone tool technology, the abundance of flint in the north-east of Ireland and the restricted distribution of the rock types preferred for the manufacture of axes, most notably porcellanite mined at Tievebulliagh near Cushendall, and on Rathlin, must have allowed for the development of specialist axe producers and early industries. The Irish Stone Axe Project has demonstrated that porcellanite axes accounted for over 50% of Irish stone axe production in the Neolithic and have been found right across Britain and Ireland (see Corrstown and Ballyharry, Chapter 1). Pitchstone from western Scotland and volcanic tuff from Great Langdale in Northern England were also imported into Ireland suggesting similar axe-producing industries operating in Britain in the Neolithic.

By the time of the Bronze Age there was an even greater disparity in the distribution of raw materials namely the copper, tin and gold ores required for the manufacture of metal tools, weapons and ornaments. Irish Bronze Age copper mines have been identified in Counties Kerry and Cork while tin, smelted with copper to produce the alloy bronze, was probably imported from Cornwall, as no significant tin source in Ireland has been identified. Recent analysis has been carried out on the compositional variation of gold from a variety of natural sources compared with that in prehistoric gold objects. This study indicates a strong correlation between gold used in the Early Bronze Age and gold sourced from the western Mourne Mountains and upper Bann River. If these were the primary (and exclusive?) sources of the basic ingredients for bronze and gold production in Ireland at this time then the evidence for the use and production of metal objects right across the island, including the very north (see Corrstown and Ballyprior Beg, Chapter 1; and Killymoon, this chapter), implies trade and exchange over long distances. How this was organised and how the materials were distributed is uncertain but those who managed and controlled these networks must have been wealthy and powerful. Iron ores are more widespread and are found as bog ores and rock outcrops though as with other ores, the acquirement and distribution of iron ores would also have needed organisation.

The achievements of the bronzesmiths and goldsmiths in Late Bronze Age and Iron Age Ireland, their technical skills and copious output, imply that there must have been full-time specialist craftsmen. It is also likely that there were permanent workshops and perhaps metalworking centres, as large quantities of the ore and charcoal would have been required for smelting, as well as an array of specialist tools. Arguably the most impressive range and quality of objects manufactured in the Irish Bronze Age were the ornaments of gold. Unfortunately the vast majority of these are poorly provenanced. The discovery of the Killymoon ornaments (see below in this chapter) found in a secure, dated context is therefore noteworthy.

Industrial activity on a small scale is found on sites throughout the Medieval period. This is represented in the main by iron working debris along with evidence for domestic pottery production, spinning and weaving of cloth, woodworking and bone-working, and the working of leather. Artefacts recovered from the ninth-century phase of activity at Dunnyneill Island for example (see Chapter 3) demonstrated that a wide range of craft activities was being undertaken, including metalworking. From the River Blackwater, on the Tyrone-Armagh border, a collection of broken bits of ecclesiastical metalwork and lead weights was recovered. These have been interpreted as the lost property of a metalworker of around AD 900 (see Chapter 3). Specialised craft production has also been found on excavations of certain monastic sites, secular ringforts and crannogs indicating that the Church and the upper levels of society patronised artisans and specialist craft workers in Early Medieval Ireland.

The processing of foodstuffs also changed from small-scale drying and grinding of grains and cereals – as witnessed by the hand querns found at Killymoon (see below in this chapter) – to the widespread use of drying kilns and mills by around AD 600. The harnessing of tidal power at Nendrum (also discussed in this chapter) represents a major technological innovation in Early Medieval Ireland.

Towns in Ulster developed under the earldom established by John de Courcy in 1177 and their prime purpose was trade and commerce through markets and ports. Markets stimulated the growth of industries and contemporary industries included potteries and stone masonry, though the Irish economy was still primarily agricultural. Following the Plantation in Ulster there was increased commercialisation of the economy, in particular in Belfast. In the 1630s, documentation indicates the presence of ironworks, breweries and tanneries in Belfast while a 1791 map illustrates the town's rapid development with numerous foundries, a flour mill, glasshouses, a paper mill and other industries. By the mid nineteenth century it was a major industrial city.

Over recent years a number of archaeological investigations, carried out in advance of redevelopment, have uncovered the vestiges of some of these seminal industries of the early modern town of Belfast. These excavations have also been highly visible due to their scale and location even if precisely what was being uncovered, obscured amongst shuttering, water pumps and the infamous Belfast sleech, was not always clear to the onlooker. As the images included here show, the sites are also often best observed and understood from the air. Excavations summarised in this chapter include the brickworks at Annadale in south Belfast and the glass works at Ballymacarett located between the River Lagan and the Short Strand. The remains of other Belfast industries also uncovered over recent years include pits and waste from tanneries in and around Waring Street and Cotton Court, while much ceramic material and kiln furniture relating to the Belfast Potthouse (which dates to around 1697–1725) have been found on Waring Street and Hill Street, though as yet, not the kiln itself.

Many of the distinctive industrial buildings and purpose-built factories from the eighteenth and nineteenth centuries have been demolished. Although only the foundations survived at Annadale and Ballymacarett, the sheer scale of the structures at these two sites, accompanied by contemporary photographs, illustrations, histories and descriptive accounts, demonstrate how different Belfast would have looked only a few centuries ago. The addition of the accompanying fumes, smoke and smells would have meant life in the industrial town presented a very different sensual experience to that felt today.

Gold, grain and flame: questions from Killymoon

Declan Hurl

In the hot summers of the early 1990s in a rolling green field on a raised inter-drumlin bog near Cookstown in County Tyrone, a farmer noticed that his cattle were dislodging stone artefacts out of the dried peat. He contacted archaeologists in the NIEA in Belfast who visited the site to find saddle querns – old hand querns used for grinding grain – hammer stones, polished stone axes and flint tools scattered around the eroded areas. Specialists from Queen's University Belfast removed a sample of the peaty soil for radiocarbon analysis and this returned a date in the tenth century BC – the Late Bronze Age. An excavation was initiated several years later in 1995 to investigate the nature and extent of the site (Plate 4.1).

Plate 4.1 General view of the site at Killymoon during excavation (NIEA).

The site, in Killymoon demesne, was defined by a thin but extensive layer of ash (23m by 12m) which sealed three baked mounds. The central mound was the largest (3.5m by 2.5m and 0.5m high), and it was set in a depression in the peat. It was made up of a dozen alternating layers of baked clay and charcoal, like a nest of upturned bowls, set on a dome of sandstone slabs. Of the other two mounds, the southern one (2.5m in diameter) had four layers of charcoal and baked clay. Again there was a setting of stones at the base of the mound though in this case they were of rough limestone blocks. The northern mound, at 2m in diameter, was the smallest. It was also composed of four layers of charcoal and baked clay which rested on the burnt remains of several small planks.

It would appear that whatever processes were being carried out at the site, they were occurring repeatedly, directly on top of earlier deposits. The by-products of these activities, principally grey ash and charcoal both of which extended right across the site, built up the mounds even further. On the peeling away of these layers, no evidence was found for features such as flues or channels which might have provided some clues as to what was being carried out at the site. The high temperatures which must have been generated, however, would suggest a repeated industrial process rather than a domestic one.

Associated with and adjacent to all three mounds were deposits of ash and baked clay similar to the material making up the mounds. Lying on the peat beneath one such deposit and to the west of the large central mound, two gold objects were found. These comprised a 'dress-fastener' and a smaller 'sleeve-fastener', both made of solid curving rods of gold with circular, flattened disc-like ends, or terminals (Plates 4.2 and 4.3). As with many other such examples, the larger object, which was probably a bracelet, was plain and unadorned; the smaller one, on the other hand, was delicately decorated with longitudinal grooves on the outside of the body and criss-cross ornamentation below the terminals. This style of goldwork, the production of solid gold objects, dates to the Late Bronze Age.

The discovery of the gold objects was important for a number of reasons. First, another similar undecorated 'dress-fastener' (now in the National Museum of Ireland) was previously found within a rough alder box from the same townland. Little is known of the context of deposition of the earlier finds save that they were retrieved from a bog in Killymoon during the construction of the adjacent railway in the nineteenth century. Second, the precise age of such artefact types was then not known as all previous discoveries had been circumstantial, that is to say not found on archaeological investigations. In the 1995 excavation, samples taken from the ground surface on which the gold objects were lying and from the layers sealing them, gave radiocarbon results dating to the thirteenth to early twelfth century BC. Third, these objects were the last to be processed as 'treasure trove' in Northern Ireland, as the new Treasure Act was passed in 1996. They are now in the Ulster Museum.

Plate 4.2 Gold 'dress fastener' and smaller 'sleeve fastener', as found at Killymoon (NIEA).

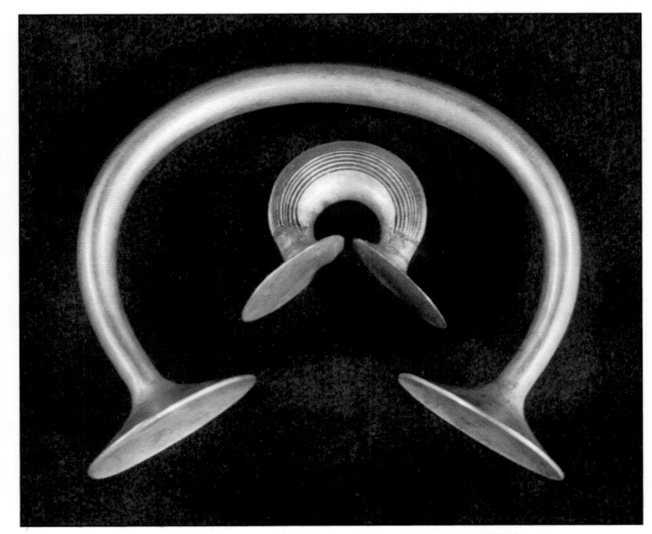

Plate 4.3 The gold objects after conservation (NIEA).

The purpose of the site remains unknown. Despite the presence of the three burnt mounds, there was no evidence that the casting of gold or other metalworking was being carried out. It is hard to imagine that the gold objects were accidentally dropped and left behind without any efforts being made to recover them. If not, were they deliberately buried either using this place as an improvised hiding place and never retrieved, or, as a deliberate votive offering? As is so often the case on archaeological sites, it is easier to explain what happened than why it happened.

A large assemblage of Bronze Age artefacts was recovered during the excavation. None of these was quite as spectacular as either of the two gold objects, although they are arguably as important and informative. Lying on the grey ashy soil at the northern edge of the site a small bronze socketed axe was recovered, and found dotted around it were stone spindle whorls (for spinning wool), polished stone axes, saddle querns, rubbing stones, hammer stones, and a considerable quantity of coarse pottery. Two clay moulds, incomplete, were also found; one for a stick pin and the other for a spearhead. There were organic finds as well which included human and animal hair, both loose and braided, and woollen twine and cloth (Plate 4.4). Whether they had a connection with activities on the site, or were simply lost over the years of use, is not known.

Plate 4.4 Magnified view of woollen cloth from Killymoon (NIEA).

Also overlying the upper layer of peat were substantial spreads of charcoal and, surprisingly, charred barley. Usually if the remains of such cereals are discovered they amount to no more than a few handfuls, whereas the barley found at Killymoon survived in deposits up to 0.2m thick and spread out over an area 2m in diameter. It is unlikely that the burning process that produced the charred barley was the same as that behind the production of the baked clay mounds, as the temperatures that would be sufficient to bake the clay would certainly have consumed the grain.

It is still not clear what activities were being carried out at the Killymoon site in the Late Bronze Age that produced the baked mounds and the extensive deposits of ash and charcoal. There was no sign of metalworking residue associated with them, and the heat which they generated would have been too high if the purpose was just to dry or even char the barley. Nonetheless, saddle querns, probably associated with the processing of barley, were found at the site – the very objects which caught the farmer's eye and started the investigations in the first place.

Further reading

Hurl, D.P. 1996 'Killymoon: new light on the Bronze Age', *Archaeology Ireland* 9(4), 24–27.

The monastic tide mills of Nendrum

Thomas McErlean

One of the most spectacular and remarkable discoveries in Irish archaeology of recent years occurred in 1999 at Nendrum monastery on Strangford Lough. Excavations carried out on the foreshore below the Early Medieval monastery uncovered what, at the time of writing, is Ireland's earliest mill constructed in the years AD 619–621 (Plates ii and 4.5). The mill was powered by the tides and has the further distinction of being so far the earliest dated tide mill in the world.

Plate 4.5 View of Nendrum from the north showing the monastic ruins, the site of both mills under excavation (middle left of photograph) in 1999 and the visible remains at low tide of the dams of the first and second tide mills on the foreshore below the monastery (NIEA).

The mill was built to service the Early Medieval monastery at Nendrum, which was at its height as a monastic establishment in the seventh and eighth centuries AD. As Nendrum is situated on a tidal island devoid of freshwater streams, the monks turned to the latent energy of the twice-daily rise and fall of the tides, which washed the shore at the bottom of the monastic enclosure, to power their mill. Accurate dating by dendrochronology was made possible by the survival of many of the oak timbers used in the massive dam of the tidal millpond. This mill appears to have been a great success and may have served the monastery for over 150 years. However, during its working life it is likely to have become run down and defects in its design must have emerged. This, combined with advances in mill technology, may have made it seem increasingly out of date, with the result that the old mill was decommissioned and a grand new mill was built in about AD 789. This later mill was found in a superb state of preservation and provides one of the most complete examples of an Early Medieval mill discovered in Ireland or elsewhere.

Ancient watermills fall into two categories classified by the rotational plane of their waterwheels. These are the vertical-wheeled watermill and horizontal-wheeled watermill. Both of the Nendrum tide mills (along with the overwhelming number of other early Irish mill discoveries) are of the horizontal-wheeled type and Figure 4.1 illustrates how this type of mill functioned. The defining characteristic of the horizontal-wheeled mill is that its wheel rotated in a horizontal plane. The transmission of power from the waterwheel to the millstones is performed by a vertical shaft and is therefore direct and does not involve any gearing, unlike that required by the vertical type. The mechanism needs only two bearings, one at the base of the waterwheel and the other in the hole at the centre of the lower millstone. The mill building consisted of two storeys, an upper storey housing the grinding apparatus (the millhouse) and the lower storey or undercroft which housed the waterwheel assembly (the wheelhouse - Plate 4.6). The waterwheel with its shaft was positioned directly below the millstones, which were on the floor of the millhouse above. The other major components of the mill complex were the millpond and its dams and sluice gates, the penstock or flume – a chute shaped like a trough which channelled the water to the waterwheel – and the tail-race which channelled the water away from the wheel. In contrast to all other known examples of penstocks of previously discovered horizontal-wheeled mills, which are of wood, that of the second mill at Nendrum was of stone (Plate 4.7).

Figure 4.1 Conjectural reconstruction drawing by James Patience of how a horizontal-wheeled type mill functioned based on the evidence of the second mill (Mill 2) excavated at Nendrum (NIEA).

Plate 4.6 General view of the Nendrum wheelhouse (Mill 2) under excavation with scaffolding supporting the mouth of the penstock (NIEA).

Plate 4.7 Back wall of the wheelhouse (Mill 2) showing the orifice façade of the penstock (NIEA).

The excellent survival of many of the features of the second mill, Mill 2, made it possible to make a reasonably reliable assessment of its annual energy capacity and more speculatively, to estimate a figure for its annual output of milled grain. If the mill worked at full capacity a figure in the region of 50 tonnes of coarsely milled barley is suggested. The amount of more finely milled flour would have been below this figure but still substantial. There is little difficulty in accepting, therefore, that Mill 2 was more than capable of supplying a sizable monastic community with all its milled grain requirements for bread and other cereal-based foodstuffs. Furthermore, it can be envisaged that it was capable of producing a surplus above what was consumed at the monastery. If production did go beyond the means of the community it opens up the possibility that the monastery was engaged in trading meal and flour.

Harnessing the power of the tides was not a simple matter. It involved great technological difficulties and represented a major investment in material and labour. It is probable that, at the time of construction, both mills were at the cutting edge of contemporary technology. It appears likely that the builders incorporated the latest innovations in water-powered milling and among the many interesting aspects of the excavation was detecting the technological advances of the period. Due to the survival of parts of the waterwheels of both mills, for example, it was possible to demonstrate that during the seventh and eighth centuries a considerable improvement in waterwheel design took place.

The excavations at Nendrum have provided a fascinating window into the Irish Early Medieval world with evidence revealed on hydraulic engineering and mill technology of the seventh and eighth centuries. The excavations have also provided further insights into the organisation of an early Irish monastery and generated new information on many themes. Among these is how former coastal communities exploited the resources offered by the maritime environment. We are already well aware of many aspects of early maritime heritage such as the harvesting of fish, shellfish and seaweed and the ability to navigate the sea, but it is rather more surprising to discover that the tides were harnessed for milling at such an early date.

The results of the excavations have attracted considerable international attention as information on early milling is of universal interest. The invention of the flour-mill and the mechanical use of waterpower with its rapid adoption in the early centuries of the first millennium AD were one of the great advances in the history of technology. It had a direct impact on food processing, relieving a large section of the population of their laborious manual daily grind of grain for bread. Though designed in the seventh and eighth centuries, the Nendrum tide mills have a particularly modern appeal. The wheel has come full circle, and sources of green energy latent in wind and tides are once again seen as viable alternative power sources that constitute renewable environmental assets.

Further reading

McErlean, T. and Crothers, N. 2007 *Harnessing the tides: the Early Medieval tide mills at Nendrum monastery, Strangford Lough*. Belfast: TSO Ireland (NIEA).

The Ballymacarett glasshouses in East Belfast

Martin Keery

The growth of industry in Belfast had been gathering pace in the late eighteenth century and nowhere was this better represented than by the development of the Ballymacarett townland, located on the south bank of the River Lagan in east Belfast (Figure 4.2). This land was ideally suited for industry since it was then, for the most part, undeveloped. The many industries that were

Figure 4.2 Excerpt from J.H. Connop's Bird's Eye View of Belfast showing the Ballymacarett glasshouses. The largest of the conical glasshouses is Smylie's glasshouse and Edward's glasshouse is located immediately south of it on the same side of the road (reproduced with permission of the Linen Hall Library, Belfast).

established there around this time included iron foundries, potteries, a vitriol works, a ropeworks and glassworks. There were at least three glass-making buildings or 'glasshouses' at Ballymacarett and the sites of two of these fell within an area of recent redevelopment and have been subject to archaeological investigation. One was excavated in 2008 and is the focus of this article, and a second was investigated in spring 2009.

Plate 4.8 Engraved blown-moulded glass decanters, dated to around 1780, and all marked on base 'Benjamin Edwards, Belfast' (photograph reproduced courtesy of the Trustees of National Museums Northern Ireland).

The glassworks excavated at Ballymacarett in 2008 belonged to John Smylie and Co. and were located west of Benjamin Edward's earlier glasshouse, erected in 1776 (excavated in 2009 – Plate 4.8), on what was then the shore of the Lagan. John Smylie began the construction of his glasshouse in 1784 with the support of 12 financial backers, all of whom contributed £100 to start up the business. The glassworks began producing glass bottles in 1786 and by 1788 had expanded into manufacturing plate and crown window glass. The standard glasshouse of the latter half of the eighteenth century was a distinctive brick-built cone (Plate 4.9). These were designed to provide an up-draught for the centrally positioned glass furnace or kiln, while also providing cover and a large work space for the glass workers. At the time of its erection, Smylie's glasshouse at Ballymacarett was the largest in Great Britain and Ireland standing over 36m high and 22m wide at its base.

Plate 4.9 A photo by A.R. Hogg of one of the Ballymacarett glasshouses taken in January 1930 (reproduced courtesy of the Trustees of National Museums Northern Ireland: H10/08/22(Y1588)).

By 1792 Smylie and Co.'s business had expanded and his original glasshouse was now used solely for the manufacture of window glass with a second glasshouse constructed nearby for the production of bottles. Production ceased at Smylie's two glasshouses in 1800 and in 1809 Smylie and Co. advertised that they were willing to receive offers on the entire site or for it to be let in subdivisions. Benjamin Edwards Jr. purchased the site but by 1823 Smylie's glasshouse is recorded as being unoccupied. Several decades later in 1881, the Sirocco Works (by which name the site is

Plate 4.10 Aerial photo of the Ballymacarett excavations, taken in 2008, with the circular foundations of the Smylie glasshouse clearly visible towards the centre. The site is bounded by the Short Strand to the left of the photograph and Bridge End to the bottom (Gahan & Long Ltd).

now commonly known), was established on the site. It produced most of the world's tea drying machinery and latterly, ventilation systems and ship propellers. Smylie's glasshouse stood until October 1937 when it was destroyed during a storm.

The remains uncovered in 2008 consisted of Smylie and Co.'s primary glasshouse and associated structures, Benjamin Edwards Jr.'s tobacco pipe complex, a bottle stopper kiln and later Victorian buildings. The archaeological remains of the Smylie glasshouse consisted of a large double-walled circular structure (Plate 4.10). The inner stone wall had a wide base which became narrower as it rose from the ground giving the glasshouse its cone shape. The outer wall was vertical and was constructed of red brick above a stone foundation. It is assumed that this would not have risen more than a storey. There was a total of five breaks through this outer wall, two of which marked the entrances in the east and west. These corresponded with breaks in the inner wall allowing access to the furnace area. The third and fourth breaks were in the north and north-east of the outer wall and may have been used as access to storage areas as the inner wall was intact in both locations. The last break in the outer wall was located in the south where it conjoined ancillary buildings housing machinery. This machinery would have been used to cut glass and may have been a later addition and constructed when the glasshouse began specialising in window glass. The outer wall was mostly concentric with the inner wall except in the north-east quadrant where it flared out to twice the normal distance possibly to accommodate additional workshops.

The walls and floor of the main entrance passage within the glasshouse were constructed from red brick. The main working floor was also constructed of red bricks which overlay clay and sand layers imported to build up and raise the level of the central area. A firebox from where the furnace would have been lit was located towards the centre of the building just north of the main passage in the north-east quadrant. Adjacent to this and located centrally within the cone there would have been a circular furnace, probably domed; no trace of this survived. The furnace would have accommodated clay pots, elevated above the heat source, in which the glass was melted and accessed by the glassworkers through apertures in the furnace wall. The furnace received air from a system of flues which ran underneath the cone and the remains of two of these were uncovered but not excavated.

There are no clear references to the sources of the raw materials used in the Smylie glasshouse though it is probable that local sand was used for the production of bottle glass. No quay was located in the development area but in J.H. Connop's 1860s map of Belfast (Figure 4.2) a quay appears to be marked to the north-west of the glassworks, which are clearly visible in the illustration. The river would have been essential for the importing and exporting of goods and one documentary source makes particular reference to the importing of coal by river. Edwards had a warehouse in central Belfast in Hanover Quay where he sold his goods directly to the public.

Smylie and Co. also had another source of revenue. They sold the land that they had reclaimed using the waste products from the glassworks, thereby providing additional funds for the construction of their second glasshouse. This reclaimed ground, stretching 15m to the west of the original glasshouse boundary and also to the south and partially to the east, was represented by a mixture of clinker and clays. Reclamation continued into the nineteenth century ultimately producing the modern shoreline. Excavations in this area uncovered a number of Victorian

Plate 4.11 Floor of the bottle stopper kiln, with flues visible, at Ballymacarett (Gahan & Long Ltd).

structures that had been cut through the infill and which yielded, along with the vast quantities of clinker, small amounts of discarded window glass which presumably would have been produced at the site. Glass bottles were also recovered but there were no distinguishing marks to indicate where they had been manufactured. An article in the *Belfast Newsletter* in the late nineteenth century requested that broken and used bottles were brought to Smylie's glasshouse. This indicates that glass was recycled here and probably used as cullet which was added to the other ingredients in the clay pots in the furnace to assist the melting process.

A clay tobacco pipe works was located in the south-east of the site. This was constructed by Benjamin Edwards Jr. who is accredited with being the first clay pipe maker in Belfast in the eighteenth century. The fragmentary remains of a clay pipe kiln were excavated. A further kiln, which appears to have produced ceramic bottle stoppers, was located nearby (Plate 4.11). The remains of this kiln show that there were four flues located equidistant around the circular base and over 50 bottle stoppers both complete and fragmentary were recovered during the excavation.

A puddling pool where the clay was pulverised, processing station and a cobbled drying or storage area were also located. The processing station that was found only survived as a large sandstone block with a metal bracket inserted in the top of it but the actual mechanics of the processing have been lost. These areas are likely to be associated with both the clay tobacco pipe and ceramic bottle stopper kilns.

The excavation at Smylie's glasshouse has revealed a site of national importance. None of the Irish conical glasshouses that once existed now survive and the only other excavated example in Northern Ireland is a smaller eighteenth-century kiln at Ballycastle, adjacent to the harbour, which was excavated in 1974 and where the cone base has partially been preserved. Given that the Ballymacarett glasshouse was one of the largest examples of its kind and exported its wares globally, it is essentially tied into the history and development of Belfast.

The building of Belfast: archaeological investigations at Annadale and Castle Espie

Stephen Gilmore

In the late nineteenth century the area between the Ormeau Road and the River Lagan in south Belfast, now covered by housing, was the site of seven large brickworks (Plate 4.12). The most southerly of these was the Annadale Brick Company Limited. After its closure the works were levelled and Annadale Grammar School was built on the site. The school buildings were replaced in 2003 by housing but before the area was redeveloped, it was investigated for surviving remains from its earlier industrial past.

Documentary sources refer to brick making on the site prior to the 1830s but it was only with the opening of James Carolan's brickfield in the late 1850s that things really got going. At this stage the works were small scale with the dried bricks being fired in clamps. The Annadale Brick Company Limited first appears in the documentary sources as the lessee in 1888 and it was from this period that industrial-scale brick making began. By 1890 new buildings had been erected and a Hoffman kiln constructed costing £6,500 – equivalent in today's terms to approximately £512,732, based on the Retail Price Index. The Hoffmann continuous kiln technology was patented for brick making by a German, Friedrich Hoffmann, in 1858 and the kiln's development revolutionised lime burning and brick making on a global scale, feeding the massive Victorian expansion in housing,

Plate 4.12 R.J. Welch's photo of the Haypark Brickworks, dated September 1910. The photograph shows brick hacks (covered piles of bricks allowed to dry prior to firing) with the chimney of the Annadale Hoffmann on the left (reproduced courtesy of the Trustees of National Museums Northern Ireland: W10/62/7).

transport and industry. The structure at Annadale was 64m in diameter and 7m high with a 50m-tall chimney in its centre, making it the largest Hoffmann kiln constructed in Ireland. The kiln was circular and divided into 24 sequentially fired chambers enabling the continual firing of bricks with the surplus heat produced being used to pre-heat the next chamber. At its peak the company was manufacturing some 6.5 million bricks per year.

The 1902 Ordnance Survey map of Belfast shows the Hoffmann kiln, associated buildings of the brickworks and the clay pits surrounding the site, while later maps indicate that the first building phase of the Annadale School was constructed in the early 1950s directly over these earlier structures. When the site was being assessed prior to redevelopment in 2003, it was uncertain to what extent these earlier industrial buildings survived. Test trenching, however, established that the school had been built with shallow foundations on a concrete raft, so the potential for below-ground survival of the brickworks was good.

Excavations at the site in 2003 began within the school playground and revealed extensive lengths of walling continuing in all directions. Upon full excavation these were found to represent subsidiary structures of the brickworks complex covering an area of around 3,600m² and surviving to a height of over 6m (Plate 4.13). The building remains comprised a machine shop, three drying floors and two earlier kilns, along with a series of connecting flues for the transfer of heat. The

Plate 4.13 Aerial photo of the development site at Annadale in 2003. The circular Hoffmann kiln is located towards the centre of the photograph and associated kilns, drying floors and other buildings are located between it and the River Lagan (NAC Ltd).

drying chambers in these buildings were connected to the kilns via a network of brick-built barrel-vaulted flues. When in operation the hot gases would have been diverted along these via a series of steel shutters, controlled by chains and counterweights, and four of these were found to be still in place. The two western drying floors upon which the green (unfired) bricks were stacked were brick-built with an under-floor heating system. In part of this complex perforated copper piping had been laid, suggesting that an attempt had been made to alter the heating system from direct heat to gas firing. The later, and larger, northern drying floor was of concrete construction and was flue-gas heated while a chimney at the northern end drew the system. Rail beds running east from the eastern edge of this building range confirmed that horse drawn rail carts were used to transfer the bricks round the works and into the kilns.

Lying to the east of these buildings was the brick-built Hoffmann kiln (Plate 4.14). The green bricks would have been taken into the kiln through one of 24 openings or 'wickets', in the thick outer wall and stacked for firing in an arched passage. This was divided into a series of 24 chambers each about 4m wide, which encircled the whole kiln. This overlay a series of 24 regularly spaced brick-built arched tunnels which functioned as a radial flue system for the circulation and control of heat and gases in the subsurface structure of the kiln. The firing floor was of baked clay with the soil between the flues burnt red to a depth of up to half a metre. Coke or coal was used to fire the bricks and was added via a network of feed holes from the working platform above the firing chamber. By manipulation of the fuel and circular steel dampers (several

Plate 4.14 The excavated remains of the Hoffmann kiln; the radial flues, kiln entrances through the outer wall and central chimney base are all clearly visible (NAC Ltd).

of which were recovered) the fire could be advanced round the kiln enabling the bricks to be loaded, fired and unloaded on a continuous cycle.

The site had been stripped of most of its metal objects when it was decommissioned but a wide range of ceramic products and styles of brick were recovered including terracotta architectural mouldings (Plate 4.15) and the plaster 'negatives' used to create them, as well as hundreds of ordinary building bricks.

Plate 4.15 Example of one of the finished decorated bricks found during the excavations at Annadale (NAC Ltd).

The knowledge and experience gained at Annadale proved unexpectedly invaluable when, just three years later, a second and even more important brickworks required investigation. The Wildfowl and Wetlands Trust at Castle Espie near Comber occupies the site of a former limestone quarry, associated lime and pottery kilns, and brickworks. The only upstanding industrial buildings within the grounds are the pump house (to remove water from the clay and lime pits), gunpowder store (for the quarry), limekiln, stable block, and the ruinous pier and seawall. A major redevelopment of the grounds in 2006 included the site of the former brick kiln and this instigated, as at Annadale, a full investigation.

A County Down man, Robert Murland, purchased the eighteenth-century lime quarries and adjacent lands at Castle Espie in 1864 and just two years later work commenced on his Hoffmann kiln. Unlike the later Annadale kiln in Belfast, the Castle Espie kiln was rectangular. Work finished on the kiln in March 1867 and as Hoffmann's rectangular kiln patents were registered in Austria less than two years earlier, it suggests that Robert Murland's decision to proceed with this type of kiln was made soon after the patent registration. The construction at Castle Espie employed 25 masons, 11,000 tons of local greywacke building stone and 1,250,000 bricks for flues, firing chambers and wickets. The Hoffmann kiln was 72m long, 19m wide and 6m in height and drawn by a 52m-high chimney (Plate 4.16). The initial firing of the new kiln took place on March 18th 1867, although unfortunately Robert, the driving force behind the enterprise, died in December of the same year, leaving the works to be run by his father and brother-in-law. Just 12 years later in 1879 the works closed probably without ever turning a profit. They were sold in October 1885 and production never resumed. It is impossible to know whether Robert Murland, had he survived, could have made a success of Castle Espie; the availability of cheap brick from numerous sources closer to the major Belfast market may suggest not.

The first phase of archaeological investigation at Castle Espie took place in late August 2006 with the aim of locating and establishing the levels of survival of the Hoffmann kiln. Excavations across the centre of the kiln exposed a well-built 1.5m-diameter arched brick tunnel which ran for several tens of metres in both directions and functioned as a hot air flue. Rubble-built foundations

Plate 4.16 A contemporary photograph of the Castle Espie Hoffmann kiln, taken pre-1912 (reproduced with permission of the WWT, Castle Espie).

Plate 4.17 The base of the octagonal chimney at Castle Espie under excavation (NAC Ltd).

were visible to a depth of 2m demonstrating that they were substantially intact. The annular firing floor of the kiln was also uncovered as well as the thick stone outer wall, pierced by wickets. Trenches located at the southern and northern ends of the kiln also confirmed that the Hoffmann was an elongated octagon rather than a rectangle. A gas main, protected by stamped Castle Espie bricks, ran to the south-east of the kiln, supplying both heat and light to the works. The base of the octagonal 6.25m-diameter chimney (Plate 4.17), which had been demolished some 90 years previously, was also unveiled, as well as the brick-built flue connecting the chimney to the kiln.

Other nineteenth-century industrial buildings were also recorded. Finds of wooden vibration dampers and machine plinths suggested that one of the nearby buildings was probably the brick-making department which contained workshops for smiths and carpenters and a machine shop for the clay products. A second building had a large concrete floor and was probably a drying shed. Apart from the Hoffmann kiln and its chimney, all other features exposed during the excavations were protected and reburied. As part of the redevelopment of Castle Espie the various parts of the industrial works are being linked by a trail with interpretive boards.

The excavation of these two Hoffmann kilns, one the largest, and the other the earliest in Ireland, has provided a great deal of information on an often overlooked process of the industrial past. Annadale was also the first Hoffmann kiln to be fully excavated using archaeological techniques in the British Isles. The excavation of the site, coupled with an astonishing level of survival, has provided much information on a development that enabled the massive nineteenth-century expansion of Belfast, providing employment, habitation and an industrial base for the thousands who flocked to the city in search of a better life.

The contrast between the Annadale and Castle Espie brickworks could not have been more marked; Annadale was a large works, in the heart of a major urban brick-making complex with easy access to a booming market, while Castle Espie was a rural works, with a long and difficult sea journey to its destination market. Both kilns were also oddities for their period – the Castle Espie Hoffmann was one of the earliest examples of its type and possibly the oldest oblong Hoffmann in the British Isles, while the circular Hoffmann at Annadale was the largest of its kind built in Ireland but also constructed much later than expected, over 30 years after it was first patented. The excavated kilns suffered very different fates too, with the remains of the Annadale Hoffmann being removed to make way for a new housing development whilst the Castle Espie Hoffmann has been conserved as an important part of our industrial heritage, especially important as so few examples of any type still survive.

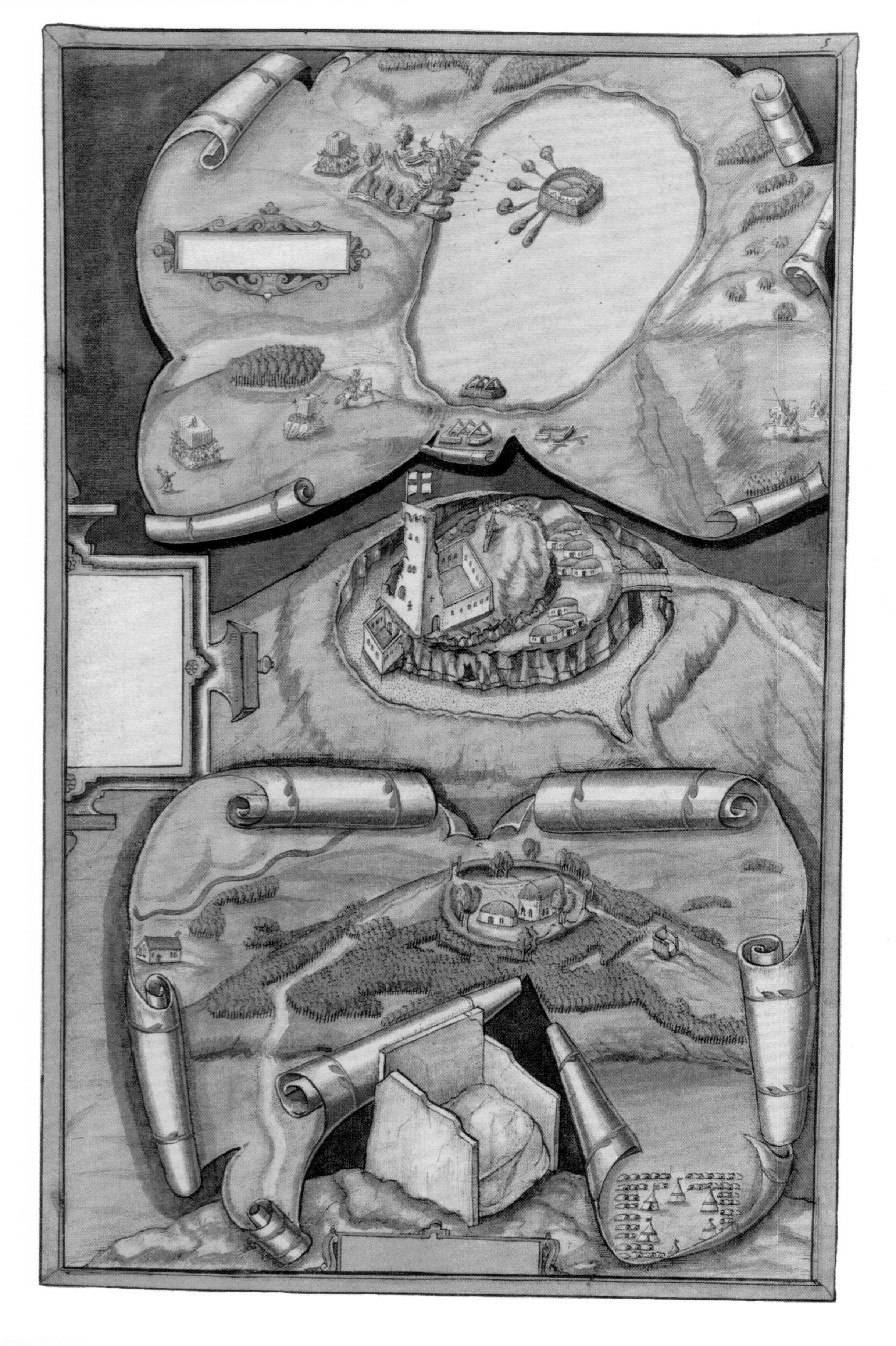

CHAPTER 5
Conflict and Fortification

Chapter 5: Conflict and Fortification

Introduction

The character of warfare is largely determined by the nature of politics and the technologies available, while the possible causes of violence are universal with competition for land and power, family feuding and conflicting beliefs being the main triggers for conflict. Archaeological attempts to reconstruct past conflict and warfare have primarily focused on fortifications and weaponry, together with historical accounts where they exist. In addition, skeletal remains displaying traumatic injuries provides perhaps the most direct and undeniable indication of interpersonal violence. Translating these bits of evidence into a coherent sense of the scale and prevalence of conflict in the past is not, however, easily done.

Limited evidence for hostilities in earlier periods in Ireland suggests more peaceful times although results from recent excavations have been used to challenge this general perception. It has been suggested that the recovery of a concentration of arrowheads found in association with evidence for the burning down of one of the houses at Ballyharry (see Chapter 1) represents direct evidence for conflict. Fire must have been one of the most effective, and feared, instruments of warfare; but fires caused accidentally would have been regular occurrences as has been recorded for domestic structures at Ballyprior Beg and Drumadoon for example (see Chapter 1). Determining the exact causes behind the archaeological remains of a burnt structure, and differentiating accidental fires from those caused deliberately through hostilities, is difficult and highly speculative.

It is probable that conflicts arose in the Neolithic, but there are no artefacts that have been found that can be definitely identified as dedicated weaponry or armour from these times in Ireland. Flint javelin heads have been found by archaeologists and when positioned on the end of a shaft they would have formed a suitable weapon. Bows and arrows would certainly have been used as weapons, as is implied by the discovery of an arrowhead found with the cremated remains of an individual in an Early Bronze Age cist at Newtownstewart (see Chapter 6). However, like javelins, their primary use was most likely for hunting. Similarly, axes and other tools could have been used as combative items but all of these would have had other primary functions in wood felling and woodworking.

It is not until the second millennium BC that purpose-made weaponry appears in Ireland with the introduction of metal halberds, daggers and spearheads and in particular in the later Bronze Age, the sword. Detailed examinations of Irish Bronze Age swords have demonstrated that large numbers show patterns of wear and notching, the latter most likely resulting from the clashing of blades. This indicates that they must have been used in combat and that they were not simply for display. The shape of swords also develops over time from a relatively short and thrusting type in the Late Bronze Age and Early Iron Age to longer swords with wider blades in the Early Medieval period to the large slashing, head-decapitating swords of the Vikings. Sword design continued to develop right through the Late- and Post-Medieval periods as demonstrated by the recovery of a variety of swords and related accessories, both Irish and imported, from a range of sites including the River Bann (see Chapter 3) and during investigations of the site of the Battle of the Yellow Ford (see below in this chapter).

Throughout the Medieval period, battles, pillaging and raiding were carried out across Ireland. The Viking raids and Anglo-Norman invasions are just part of a bigger picture of long-term small-scale warfare. This is best witnessed by the Irish annals which are full of acts of violence; dynastic rivalries and feuds, conflicts between a king and his people and other kings, much harrying and pillaging including the theft of cattle and people, naval battles and widespread arson. On land, the technology of war changed little in the first millennium AD with ordinary fighting men armed simply with the basics of an axe, a spear or sword and shield while Viking archers appear to have reintroduced the bow and arrow. From the eleventh century Irish kings maintained permanent retinues of troops, and over succeeding centuries the main development in warfare was an increasing reliance on mercenaries. Professional soldiers were employed on all sides, with Irish noblemen in the north employing Scottish gallowglass (a mercenary warrior elite) from the thirteenth century.

Given that most of the fighting undertaken in the late prehistoric and Medieval period was carried out by the landed class and aristocracy, it is not surprising that they chose to fortify their homesteads, though this may have been as much as a symbol of power and wealth as for defensive or tactical reasons. The ubiquitous monument of the mid first millennium AD in Ireland is the rath or ringfort (see discussion on Bellaghy in this chapter and Drumadoon in Chapter 1). Although these were defensive earthworks it is questionable if many were ever actually attacked or defended, or truly functioned as forts, as they had many logistical and structural weaknesses. Evidence for raiding and conflict at secular settlements at this time is, however, presented by souterrains. There has been much debate as to the purpose of these well-engineered underground passages and one of the most widely held theories is that they were built as places of refuge for those fearing capture and a life of slavery, an institution which was well established in Early Medieval Ireland (see Corrstown and Drumadoon, Chapter 1).

In the twelfth century the Anglo-Normans introduced the enduring fortifications of the landscape – the stone-built castles, as well as timber and earth castles, which survive as steep-sided mounds (mottes). The earliest of these, such as Carrickfergus Castle, were adapted and modified over the succeeding decades as the nature of warfare changed, in particular with the introduction of firearms and artillery. In the fifteenth century the dominant defensive structures were the stone-built tower-houses which employed a number of defensive features including small windows, machicolations, murder holes and stone-vaulted basements. Two excavated tower-houses included here are Castle Hill in Dungannon and Bagenal's Castle in Newry (see discussions of both in this chapter). The English and Scottish landlords who were granted estates as part of the Ulster Plantation were required to provide arms for their tenants and a bawn to defend their homes, many of which were also built with defensive attributes, typically in a Scottish or English architectural style. This concern for defence was not without cause, as signs of conflict have been recorded in the archaeological record, most notably from the 1641 rebellion when the bawn at Bellaghy (see this chapter) and castle at Lisburn (see Chapter 2) were both destroyed and which also led to the abandonment of Movanagher (see Chapter 1). Two musket balls were also found at Movanagher which may date to the uprising, as too might some of the skeletons uncovered at Bagenal's Castle several of which displayed traumatic injuries including sword wounds.

In the absence of historic documentation, such as the annals, maps and written accounts, there would be little if any evidence for battles and warfare, or the pillaging and raiding that accompanied such events. Before the widespread use of shot and cannon in Ireland from the later sixteenth century on, traces of battles in the field, such as the evidence recovered at the site of the 1598 Battle of the Yellow Ford, are minimal. Equally, the written sources and our reading of them may over-emphasise the prevalence of warfare and violence. The results from archaeological investigations, such as those sites presented here, can therefore provide further insights into the darker aspects of society and a more balanced picture of what can often be a highly political and biased subject.

Rediscovering the O'Neill tower-house and Chichester's military fort at Castle Hill, Dungannon

Emily Murray, Colm Donnelly and Paul Logue

Richard Bartlett's bird's-eye pictorial map of 1602 showing Dungannon Castle, Tullaghoge and a crannog under attack (Figure 5.1) is a wonderful and evocative glimpse of the Late Medieval world in the north of Ireland. It is an aspect of that world, however, depicted by an Englishman with certain political and symbolic intentions. For Bartlett was attached to Queen Elizabeth's army as it advanced into the heart of a landscape that had never been familiar territory, and his picture maps were designed to show the Tudor administration the nature of this newly conquered world. The illustration is a rare and valuable historic record of the contemporary landscape, in particular of Irish Late Medieval buildings and fortifications, at the turn of the seventeenth century.

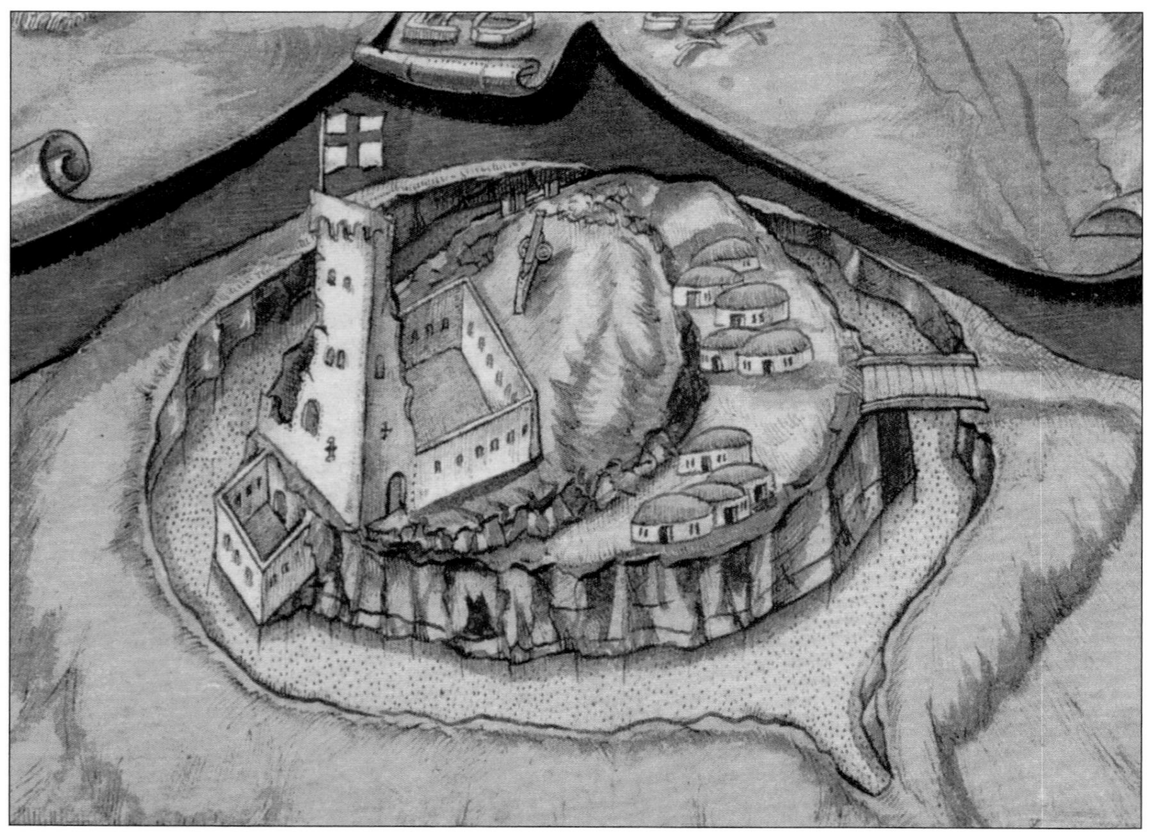

Figure 5.1 Detail from Richard Bartlett's map, of around 1602, showing the captured O'Neill Castle at Dungannon with the English flag raised on the parapet (reproduced with permission from the Board of the National Library of Ireland: MS 2656).

The castle Bartlett depicts is that of Hugh O'Neill, the 2nd Earl of Tyrone. There are a significant number of recorded incidents of intrigue and conflict from the sixteenth century that focus on Dungannon and its castle reflecting the central role of the O'Neill capital in Medieval Irish affairs. What form the O'Neill stronghold took in earlier centuries is not known though a castle at Dungannon is recorded in documents from the fifteenth century.

The only substantive evidence we have for the Gaelic castle is Bartlett's large-scale pictorial representation in which it is shown as a damaged tower-house. The illustration was most probably drafted in 1602 after the destruction of the tower-house at the behest of O'Neill himself, presumably to prevent the Crown forces gaining any advantage from his stronghold. The tower is set at a corner of a rectangular bawn and is situated towards one end of a scarped mound. The castle has an entrance at the ground floor and appears to be at least four storeys high with a machicolation visible at parapet level. At the opposite end of the mound, at the base of the rock-cut scarp, is a cluster of nine single-storeyed thatched cabins.

The Earl of Tyrone's lands, the largest autonomous Gaelic territorial unit in Ulster at that time, were forfeited to the Crown following the Nine Years' War and O'Neill's subsequent escape to the Continent in 1607 in the 'Flight of the Earls'. Three years later, under King James I's ambitious Ulster Plantation scheme, the settlement at Dungannon was granted to the new Lord Deputy, Sir Arthur Chichester, who set about building a new fort without delay. As with the Medieval castle there is just one useful illustration of the new fort, that of the surveyor Captain Nicholas Pynnar who depicts it in his 1624 map of Lough Neagh (Figure 5.2). Like Bartlett's illustration, this drawing does not include either an indication of scale or orientation although the size of the fort is recorded as being between 100 and 120 ft square (equivalent roughly to between 30m and 36.6m square) in government surveys of 1619 and 1622. The fort was accompanied by a town built 'streetways', as dictated in Chichester's patent and as illustrated by Pynnar. The apparent similarities between the tall towers depicted as the central features in both the Bartlett and Pynnar drawings would suggest that Chichester had refurbished the old O'Neill tower-house rather than embark on an entirely new construction. Indeed, in spite of the many land grants Chichester received his finances were never in a healthy state throughout his life which may have obliged him to compromise on his building schemes.

Only the name, Castle Hill, now bears witness to the impressive fortifications that once stood on the hilltop overlooking the town of Dungannon. Chichester's fort was succeeded in the late

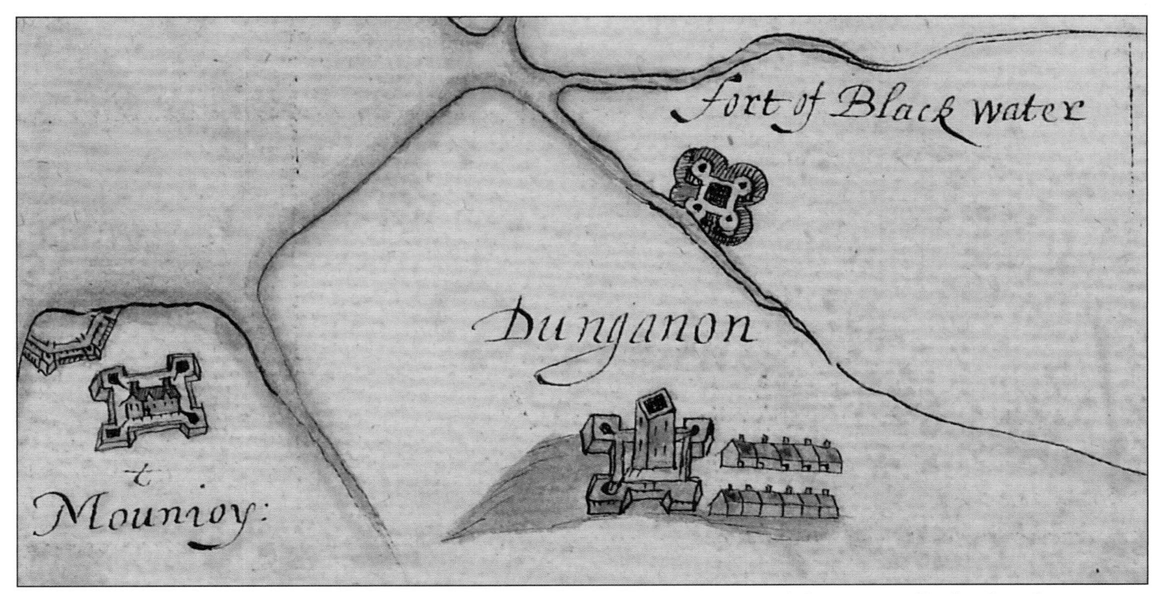

Figure 5.2 Detail from Nicholas Pynnar's map of 1624 of Lough Neagh (State of the Fortes of Ireland as they weare in the yeare 1624) showing a pictorial depiction of Chichester's fortification at Dungannon (© British Library Board. All Rights Reserved. Add. 24200 f.35b).

eighteenth century by a country house built by Thomas Knox Hanyngton, the ruins of which still stand on the hilltop, and more recently by the modern austere defences of the British Army. Although no longer visible, the earlier historic fortifications were not forgotten and in 2007, on the 400th anniversary of the 'Flight of the Earls', an excavation was carried out to try and relocate the buried remains of these early defences. Previously, in 2003, a series of 31 small test-pits had been excavated on the hilltop under the direction of Robert Chapple for Northern Archaeological Consultancy Ltd in advance of the construction of a new security fence. These keyhole excavations demonstrated the survival of structural masonry remains of possible Medieval and Post-Medieval date providing an incentive for further investigations.

The 2007 excavations were undertaken by Channel 4's *Time Team* working in close association with the NIEA and the Centre for Archaeological Fieldwork at Queen's University Belfast. The television programme was based on a three-day period of intensive fieldwork, as dictated by the long-running format of the show, although excavations continued on site for a further three weeks after the film crew left.

The proposed location of the 2007 excavation trench on the summit of Castle Hill was based on the findings of the 2003 excavations. After much effort to lift the reinforced concrete, tarmacadam and over a metre of hardcore rubble – leftovers of the army's period of occupation – mortared stones representing the top of a masonry wall were revealed (Plates 5.1 and 5.2). Further excavation of this feature exposed an angled length of wall, the plan of which suggested that it was one of the angled bastions of Chichester's fort as illustrated by Pynnar (Figure 5.2). A robbed-out section of the fort's curtain wall, bonded to and running south from the southern corner of the excavated bastion wall, was also uncovered.

Plate 5.1 The excavation trench within the hilltop compound on Castle Hill on Day 1 of the Time Team excavation (CAF).

Plate 5.2 Castle Hill under excavation (CAF).

A second length of lime-mortared masonry was also found immediately adjacent to, and to the south of, these seventeenth-century walls. Both the inner and outer faces of this earlier wall had been robbed, but at foundation level a line of dressed and coursed stones survived in their original place, indicating that the wall had an external base-batter. The relationship of this wall to those of Chichester's fort, its scale and the presence of a base-batter (an architectural signature for a Medieval tower-house), all indicate that this was the remains of one of the walls of the O'Neill's Medieval castle. Both elements of the later seventeenth-century fortification, the curtain wall and bastion, enclosed the foundation courses of the tower-house. This would suggest that Pynnar's depiction of the complex from 1624 is an accurate one and that Chichester repaired and reused the tower-house but strengthened the defences by surrounding it with a new curtain wall complete with bastions at the four corners.

The 2007 excavation also revealed that both the interior of the Medieval tower-house and the angled bastion of the later fort were infilled with stones and clay packing and surfaced with a rough stone paving which survived in places. Although the clay deposits were not excavated and independently dateable, it is probable that both clay infillings are contemporary and date to the later reuse of the site as an artillery fort. The clay infilling would have acted as a shock absorber for firing canon, and historic records indicate that the fortifications on Castle Hill were rebuilt and garrisoned with artillery in 1689.

Further reading

Chapple, R.M. 2003 'Excavations at Castle Hill, Dungannon, Co. Tyrone', *Archaeology Ireland* 17(3), 24–29.

Donnelly, C.J., Murray, E.V. and McHugh, R. 2008 'Dungannon Castle: its history, architecture and archaeology', *Dúiche Néill* 17, 11–24.

A lost castle in Newry

Noreen Cunningham

The rediscovery of Bagenal's Castle in 1996 vividly illustrates how the heritage can remain hidden, even within a bustling urban environment. The castle faded from memory as it became lost to public view and its encapsulation within the McCann's Bakery (Plate 5.3) mirrored its fall in status from prestigious dwelling to industrial unit. Now restored as a new home for Newry and Mourne Museum, the castle is a remarkable survival of a sixteenth-century fortified house (Plates 5.4 and 5.5), built at a time of transition from primarily defensible to more comfortable, residential accommodation. It is also a reminder of a turbulent time in Irish history and many of the key players of the time such as Hugh O'Neill and Lord Deputy Sidney would have politicked and parleyed within its walls.

The castle was home to the Bagenal family who played an important and influential role in Irish government and politics during the second half of the sixteenth century. In 1552 Nicholas Bagenal was granted the confiscated estates of the Cistercian abbey at Newry, along with land at Greencastle and Carlingford, by King Edward VI. It was important for the Crown that Newry should be held by a loyal and experienced individual to neutralise the threat of the powerful Gaelic lords in Ulster. As Marshall of the Army in Ireland, Bagenal was involved in various campaigns to maintain and strengthen English control, and he can be regarded as a pioneer for the later invasion and Plantation of Ulster. After Nicholas Bagenal's death in 1590, his son Henry inherited his estates and titles. During the Nine Years' War, Henry took a leading part in the military

Plate 5.3 Bagenal's Castle as it was in 1998, concealed within McCann's bakery (NIEA).

Plate 5.4 Bagenal's Castle 'in transition' in February 2005 (NIEA).

Plate 5.5 The castle in July 2007 showing its transformation and re-emergence (NIEA).

campaigns against Hugh O'Neill and in August 1598 his army was attacked and defeated at the Battle of the Yellow Ford (see below in this chapter). During the battle Henry was killed, and with his death the Bagenal sphere of influence in Irish political affairs was ended.

Although nothing was known about the physical remains of the castle, a set of drawings illustrating the building are preserved in the National Archives in London. They contain an elevation drawing (Figure 5.3) and a floor plan (Figure 5.4) of the castle and a town map (Figure 5.5), and are thought to date to around 1568. They are attributed to the English engineer and surveyor, Robert Lythe, who wrote in early 1571 that he had already completed plans of Bagenal's lands in "Coley (Cooley), Ometh (Omeath), Mourne and the Newry".

The map (Figure 5.5) shows a town divided into three parts, two of which were fortified, probably with an earthen bank and ditch. In the area marked as 'The Towne of The Newyre', Bagenal's Castle is identified as 'The New Castell'. No remains of the abbey are identified on the map, but only 20 years previously at the dissolution of the monasteries, an inquisition recorded that the abbey precincts contained a church with steeple, a chapter house, a dormitory and a hall. This may have been a deliberate omission, as a reference from around 1788 states that "...the remaining ruins of the abbey, which had, for a long time, afforded shelter only to vagrants, were levelled and enclosed for the purpose of building".

The floor plans (Figure 5.4) illustrate a rectangular building of 8.5m by 14.6m, with a doorway set towards the west wall, adjacent to an external turret housing a spiral staircase. A second, similarly sized square turret lies at one comer of the rear wall and probably functioned as a latrine block. The ground floor is divided by a substantial cross wall, with the smaller of the two rooms depicted as barrel-vaulted. A large fireplace and accompanying bread oven are depicted in the larger room built into the south wall and a mullion window is featured in the east wall. The first and second floors are each divided into two rooms, with fireplaces in the north and south walls. Mullioned windows with hooded mouldings are featured in the elevation drawing, which shows the front, west face (Figure 5.3). Other architectural features include a castellated parapet wall and chimney pairs at either gable end. Two adjacent doors are shown with machicolation, one giving entry to the ground floor of the castle, the other to the stair turret and upper rooms of the castle.

The castle was rediscovered in 1996 when it was realised that two carved stones, with ecclesiastical associations, were built into 1.5m-thick walls which, on detailed examination, corresponded well to the sixteenth-century records of Bagenal's Castle. With the rediscovery of the castle, which was rapidly scheduled by the NIEA, and the closure of McCann's Bakery, Newry and Mourne District Council took the decision to seek funding to restore the castle and the adjoining nineteenth-century warehouse as a museum. Removal of bakery machinery and surrounding buildings allowed a better examination of the structure, and from this preliminary inspection coupled with documentary research and ongoing survey, the NIEA team charted the piecemeal removal of the physical fabric from the more recent alterations. The Ordnance Survey Memoirs (1834–1836) related that the stair turret had been demolished using gunpowder around 1770, probably after the castle was subdivided into two dwelling houses. The latrine turret had also been removed, except for its north wall which had been incorporated into the warehouse building. It was during the twentieth century that the most extensive removal of wall fabric took place; the ground floor walls were altered to house bakery machinery, with the walls at the north and east removed, and the west wall reduced in width from the inside. From the first-floor level upwards, damage to the fabric was not as extensive and the walls were more or less intact.

As part of the conditions for planning permission, prior to redevelopment, Newry and Mourne District Council commissioned a series of excavations to establish the surviving extent of the

Figure 5.3 Perspective view of the front elevation of Bagenal's Castle. The cartographer and date for this drawing as well as the plans of the building and town plan are not recorded but may be the work of Robert Lythe and date to 1568 (© Crown Copyright PRO London. MPF 1/83).

castle's architectural features and how they compared to the contemporary drawings. Running in tandem with these excavations the NIEA carried out an extensive programme of recording of the standing remains. This information was used to condition the conservation work and to save as much as possible of the historic fabric of the building in its new use.

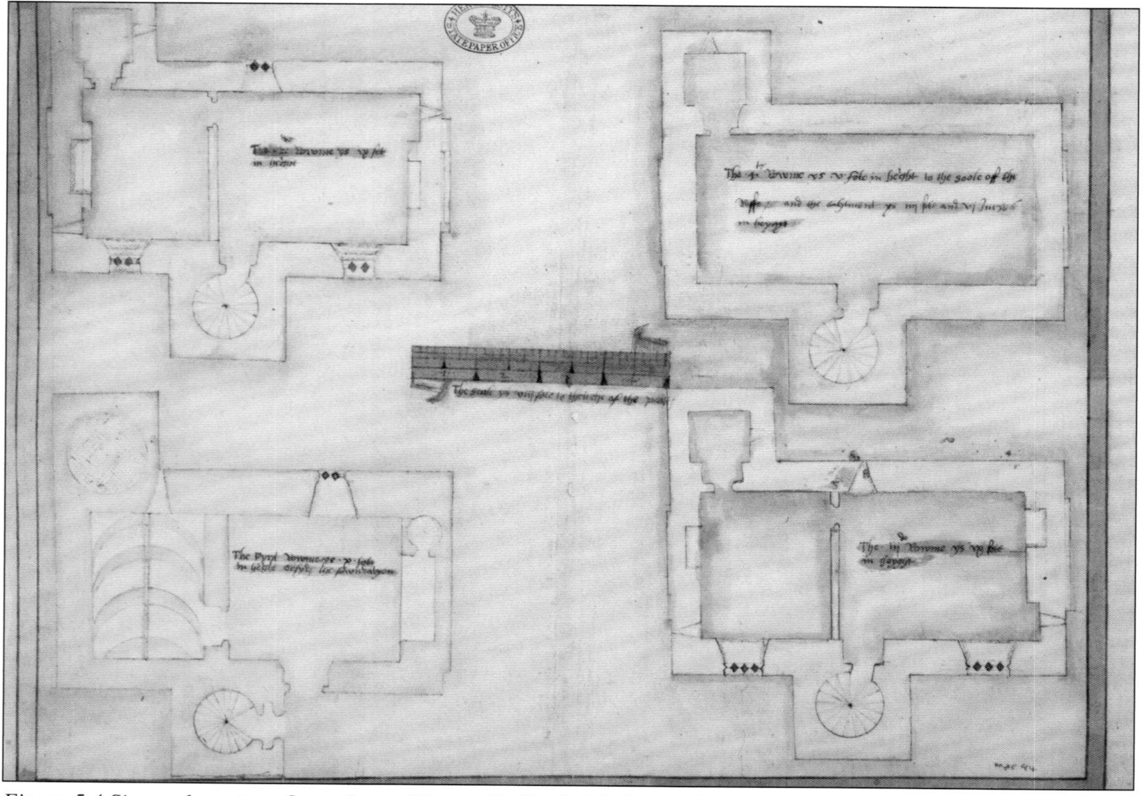

Figure 5.4 Sixteenth-century floor plans of Bagenal's Castle (© Crown Copyright PRO London. MPF 1/84).

The initial excavation of Bagenal's Castle was undertaken in 2000 to examine specific elements of the structure and to allow comparisons to be made between them and the features depicted on the contemporary drawings. A substantial wall dividing the ground floor was identified, but no trace of the stair turret was found nor was any trace of this feature discovered in 2005 when an area between the front of the west wall of the castle and the road was excavated. Evidence of later occupation of the castle was also recorded in 2000 and a period of abandonment was noted, probably dating to the latter half of the seventeenth century.

In 2003 a complete excavation of the ground floor of the castle was undertaken. These investigations totally uncovered the foundations of the dividing wall, the doorway leading into the northern room and the foundations of the north wall of the castle. A basement with stone steps had been inserted into the south room, probably dating from the eighteenth century when the castle was leased by a Newry merchant. The basement appears to have been filled in during renovations at McCann's Bakery. Stone cobbling and the base of the latrine turret were also discovered, with the former being identified as the original floor of the castle.

The most intensive phase of excavation at the site was carried out in 2005 and informed the conservation, restoration and interpretation of many of the original features of the castle. In general it was decided not to reconstruct elements that were shown on the 1568 drawings but for which no substantial physical remains existed. On this basis it was agreed not to reconstruct the stair and latrine turrets and the parapet. The most dramatic discovery of this phase of excavation was part of a cemetery just outside the north wall of the castle and within the adjoining warehouse.

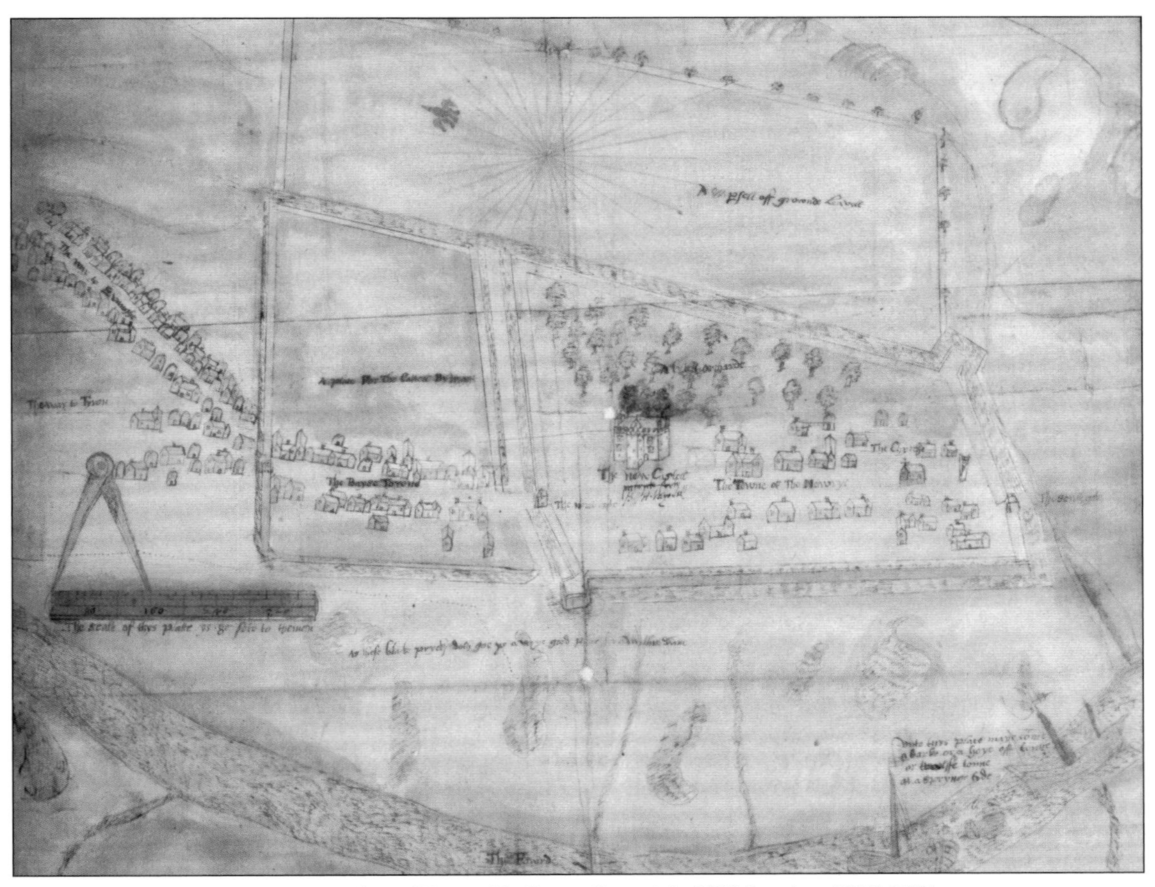

Figure 5.5 Sixteenth-century town plan of Newry (© Crown Copyright PRO London. MPF 1/82).

Thirty-three inhumation burials and other disarticulated human remains were uncovered, 15 of which could be identified as male and 10 as female. Using a combination of radiocarbon dating and stratigraphy, these were dated to between 1552 and 1660 and thus contemporary with the castle. Intriguingly at least three and possibly four individuals had suffered a violent death with one unfortunate individual having 10 separate sword wounds to the skull. The excavator has postulated that these individuals may have been Bagenal's retainers killed during one of the many battle campaigns of the period, but it is also possible that they may relate to the 1641 Rebellion when the castle was attacked.

Below the burials, foundations of a Medieval building were uncovered which the excavator has interpreted as being part of the Cistercian abbey precinct. The remains of this building had been deliberately removed and it is tempting to suggest this may have been undertaken prior to building the castle, with the robbed stone used in its construction. It is also reasonable to assume that Nicholas Bagenal would have wanted to stamp his authority by building his castle on the abbey precinct, the former centre of power in the area.

Stripping of plaster from the walls revealed many of the castle's architectural features. Crucial was the discovery of the original joist holes for the upper levels, allowing reinstatement of the sixteenth-century floor levels and interpretation of the features associated with the various floor levels. These included fireplaces, ventilation loops and doorways that led into the stair and latrine turrets on the upper levels. The original window openings were discovered on the upper levels, in some instances with the window jambs in place, with a few displaced mullion stones found in the walls. Due to past alterations, original features at ground floor level were scarce. No joist holes survived for the first floor and there was no physical indication of the barrel vaulting depicted on the 1568 floor plan. It is, however, probable that a barrel-vaulted chamber was located on the ground floor, functioning as a store room for the castle, and the substantial nature of the cross wall, which would have allowed it to support vaulting, reinforces this theory. A remarkable survival was the bread oven in the south wall, though of a rectangular outline, rather than the circular shape indicated on the floor plan. In general, the architectural features uncovered compare closely to those depicted on the sixteenth-century drawings.

Excavation and restoration has now revealed Bagenal's Castle to public gaze, and it is an important part of Newry's streetscape, linking the site's Cistercian past with its future as a modern city. Through the castle's most recent incarnation as a museum, which opened in 2007, the stories of the castle and the development of the town can now be told.

Further reading

Dawkes, G. and Buckley, L. 2006 'Bagenal's Castle, Newry: an Elizabethan tower-house and cemetery', *Archaeology Ireland* 20(4), 31–3.

O'Neill, J. 2002 'Nicholas Bagnall's castle at Newry, County Down', *Ulster Journal of Archaeology* 61, 117–124.

Investigations at the site of the Battle of the Yellow Ford

James O'Neill and Paul Logue

It was August 1598 and war had raged in Ulster for four years, with Hugh O'Neill and his confederates continuing to defy the imposition of Elizabethan rule. The English policy of placing forts deep in enemy territory had led to the Irish laying siege to an isolated fort on the banks of the River Blackwater. Loathe to lose the fort to the 'barbarous' Irish, the Dublin authorities sent a relief force, under the command of Sir Henry Bagenal, to break the blockade and relieve the fort. O'Neill was determined not to allow this to go uncontested.

Bagenal had drawn together 3,500–3,700 infantry and 350 horsemen for the journey to the Blackwater valley. They were conventionally armed and equipped for a Tudor army of the period, with a core of armoured pike-men supported by musketeers and caliver-men. As was also common for all Tudor armies in Ireland, a significant proportion were Irish who were armed and equipped and fought in the English manner. The army's mission was to protect the convoy of supplies and reinforcements over the six miles from Armagh to the beleaguered garrison. Bagenal and his men set out early on the morning of the 14th of August, six infantry regiments marching one after the other, with contingents of horse supporting the front and rear of the column. The force was engaged on the flanks by Irish shot almost immediately after breaking camp. As they crossed the Callan River, delays started to extend the column, causing gaps between the advancing regiments to widen. Although subject to continuous fire, the lead regiment rashly pushed ahead of the main body with whom Bagenal journeyed. After crossing a fording point through the bog ('the bog ford'), the advance regiment eventually came to a long trench bisecting their route. As it was not defended, their commander chose to cross the trench and to move on to the final hill before the Blackwater. What they did not yet realise was that they had blundered into a killing zone; the unseen Irish massed around them, awaiting the order to strike. Bagenal's advance

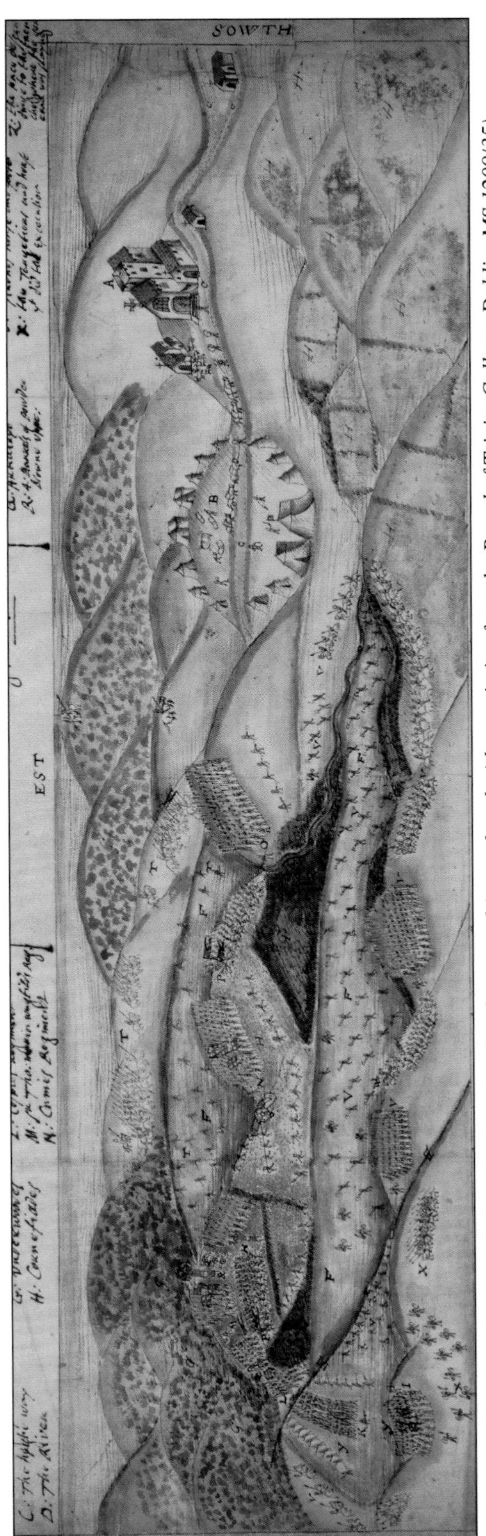

Figure 5.6 Map of the Battle of Yellow Ford, undated and unsigned (reproduced with permission from the Board of Trinity College, Dublin. MS 1209/35).

was hampered by his single heavy cannon, which was continually getting stuck and was consequently abandoned. His regiment crossed the bog ford and took position on a hill overlooking O'Neill's trench. Bagenal's regiments were hotly engaged on all sides and he was rapidly losing contact with his trailing units. On the hill ahead, O'Neill unleashed his cavalry and swordsmen on the leading regiment, tearing holes into it. Cut off from support by the trench to its rear, the lead regiment dissolved into a rout of panic stricken fugitives. Bagenal tried to move to their aid, but before he could cross the trench he fell lifeless from his horse, killed by a shot to the head. A new horror was visited on the luckless English army when several barrels of gunpowder in the baggage, possibly 200 pounds, exploded in their midst, sowing yet more death and confusion in their now dishevelled ranks. The second in command that day, Sir Thomas Maria Wingfield, took charge and organised the retreat. Contrary to his orders, two trailing regiments launched an impetuous counter attack across the bog, which would have resulted in their annihilation if they had not been recovered by the prompt action of Wingfield, who rescued 500 men from the slaughter. The battered remnants of the relief force made it to Armagh, where they negotiated their return to Newry on condition that the fort on the Blackwater was surrendered. Of the army that set out, just over 2,000 men made it to the relative safety of Newry. Around 1,800 never made it there; 300 deserted to O'Neill, including two Englishmen, and the bodies of a further 1,500 rest to this day in undiscovered graves on the battlefield.

Because of the nature of violence found on the battlefields of early modern Ireland, the comprehensiveness and veracity of written material cannot be solely relied upon. The memory of an individual was limited by the simple fact that he was only one person in an event involving thousands of participants. Lines of sight were blocked by terrain, and the predominance of firearms using black powder, producing prodigious amounts of smoke, rapidly reduced visibility. Witnesses' ability to conceive of the events as they unfolded around them was therefore limited. There are also psychological reasons why eyewitness evidence during combat can be unreliable. Combat is a traumatic event for everyone involved. When the event has passed and the soldiers have recovered from their heightened emotional state, they cannot remember all that they did or saw during battle. Worse still, what is recalled is generally the most notable or distressing snapshots which tend not to preserve any sense of chronology or context. English accounts of the battle too rarely agree, and some officers appeared to be recounting entirely separate events. There was the ever present possibility that in the aftermath of a catastrophic defeat, surviving officers attempted to fabricate accounts to avoid blame for the disaster. With written evidence of battle susceptible to distortion, testimony can be substantiated utilising the complementary tools of historical geography and archaeology.

The link between the physical geography of Armagh and the battle fought within it is unavoidable. Though the landscape has been altered by farming and development, the underlying morphology of the battlefield has remained surprisingly unchanged. Using contemporary late sixteenth- and early seventeenth-century maps (Figure 5.6) in conjunction with the modern Ordnance Survey maps of the area, it is possible to recreate the terrain at the time of the battle (Plate 5.6). Eyewitness accounts can also be compared to identify fixed geographic points within the narrative of the battle. It seems certain that the English had travelled on the east bank of the Callan and had crossed the river some distance to the north of Armagh. The heavy infantry formations of the English could not manoeuvre through bog-land and, because the road had been blocked by O'Neill, they therefore had to confine themselves to travelling along firm high ground. If the marshy areas are eliminated from the possible route Bagenal and his men took, the line of advance through the Armagh countryside can be reduced to a narrow corridor of hills running north to the Callan, then north-west to the Blackwater. It is also recorded that the garrison of the

Plate 5.6 Annotated photo showing the site of the Battle of the Yellow Ford as it is today (J. O'Neill).

Blackwater fort had seen the lead English regiment at the top of a hill. This hill has been identified as Mullyleggan Hill close to the Blackwater River and marks the farthest point of the Crown army's advance that day.

With the battleground defined and with the consent of the landowners, a series of licensed metal detector surveys were instigated with the help of the Banbridge and District Metal Detecting Club. This involved a systematic survey for artefacts relating to the battle; modern metal objects such as iron plough bits and aluminium cans were not retained. Fortunately firearms that discharged lead bullets were the main weapons used by the Irish and English troop, therefore the distribution of lead shot could be used as the primary battlefield indicator. Two areas were targeted for examination; the area of the bog ford at the Annahagh Road, and the western slopes of Drumcullen hill, on the edges of Bagenal's central position and near the site of O'Neill's trench. Work at Annahagh unearthed a linear distribution of caliver shot running parallel to the line of the English advance. Located on the edge of the bog, it represents outgoing English fire impacting around the Irish skirmishers harassing the column from the south. A damaged bronze sword chape – the metal end of a scabbard – was found at the bog ford, indicating hand-to-hand fighting in this area. The investigations around Drumcullen revealed a very different shot pattern than at the ford. The bullets were clustered at the base of the slopes representing a more intense fire-fight. Found within this concentration was a sword or dagger pommel broken off in the bloody melee that developed around the trench.

The results and interpretation above detail only a small preliminary investigation into the potential of one battle. We must remember that over 1,500 men were killed that day, most of whom remain undiscovered in the rolling countryside between Armagh and Blackwatertown.

Further reading

Logue, P. and O'Neill, J. 2007 'The battle of the Yellow Ford', *Dúiche Néill* 16, 62–83.

The bawn at 'Vintners Towne'

Nick Brannon

An unusual lottery took place in London on December 17th 1613. King James I had cajoled and persuaded the major London livery companies to invest in the colonisation of north-west Ulster, by 'planting' British colonists, building settlements, introducing the Protestant faith and reforming agricultural practice. James' purpose was to subdue the native Irish and transform the landscape. The lands of the newly created county of Londonderry had been mapped and divided. A lottery was to determine which London company would be allocated which parcel of land. The Vintners Company (its name derives from 'Wine Tonners' and its coat of arms includes three wine barrels) was allocated over 32,000 acres in the south-east of the new county, north-west of Lough Beg.

The Vintners Company determined to build their main settlement, Vintners Towne, at Bellaghy, but their agent Henry Jackson had made little initial progress by 1616. John Rowley, the tenant who succeeded him in the task, died in 1617. His partner Baptist Jones (previously involved with the Salters Company Plantation) took over the lease and progressed rapidly, as shown by a surveyor's report in 1619 stating that Jones had built "a Bawn of Brick and Lime…with two round Flanckers and a good Rampart" with "two good Houses" inside the bawn, and a village of "10 good English houses". Knighted by July 1621, Jones continued his labours, and Sir Thomas Phillips' comprehensive report of 1622 gives measured descriptions of Bellaghy bawn and 15 houses in the village, with a newly built church and a double-wheeled watermill, illustrated by a picture-

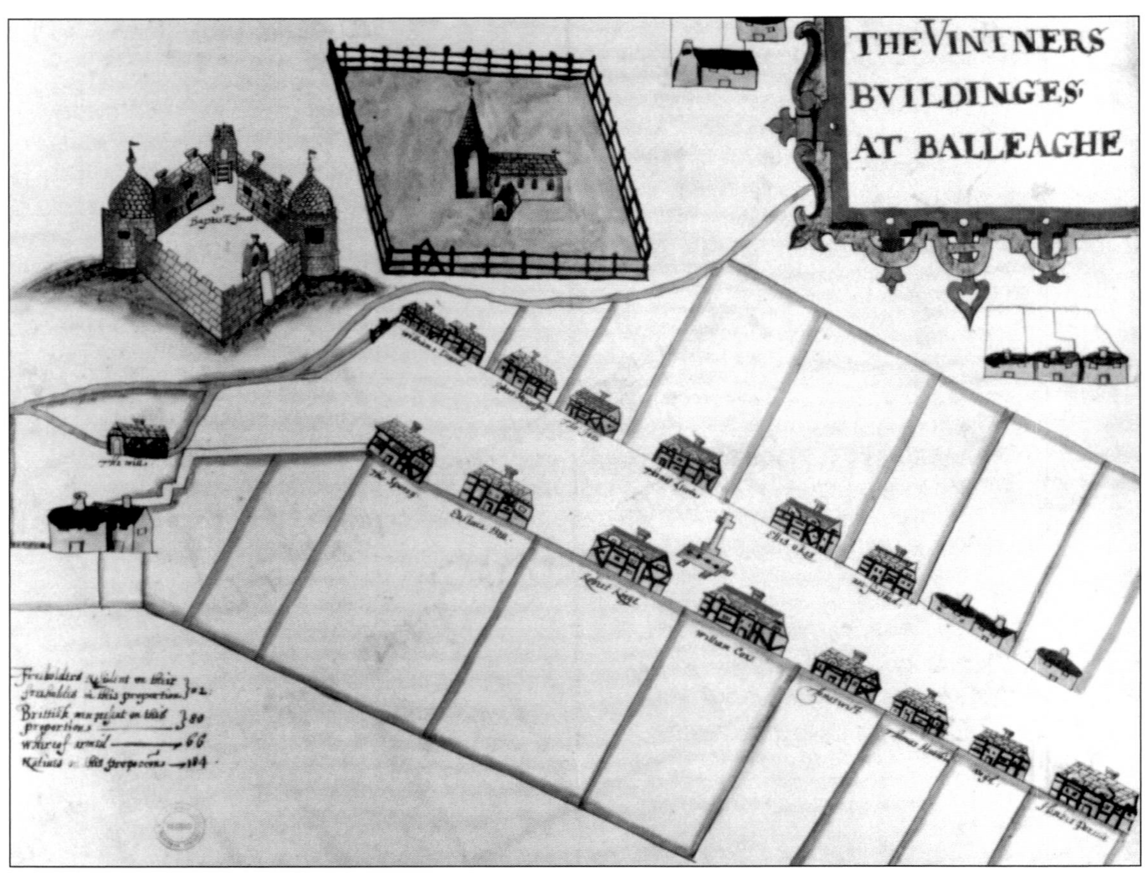

Figure 5.7 Thomas Raven's 1622 picture-map of Bellaghy (A Plat of the Vintners Buildings) showing the bawn overlooking the village (reproduced courtesy of Lambeth Palace Library. Carew Manuscript: MS634 73v-74).

map drawn by Thomas Raven. This false aerial perspective drawing, with colour coding denoting building materials (brick, tile, slate, timber and thatch) and naming the inhabitants of the dwellings shows the bawn dominating the village (Figure 5.7).

After Jones' death in 1623, his widow married Henry Conway, who as leaseholder was living in the bawn in 1641 at the time of the Ulster Rising. The native Irish, under the command of Sir Phelim O'Neill, brought about the burning of most of the village, and the siege, surrender and destruction of the bawn. Conway and the Bellaghy villagers took refuge in Carrickfergus.

The later seventeenth century saw the bawn reoccupied and undergoing physical change, under the tenancy of Viscount Massereene. Subsequently it was acquired in the eighteenth century by William Connolly, later Speaker of the Irish House of Commons, and further physical changes were wrought. Baptist Jones' houses were demolished, and a large Georgian house was built. Accounts from 1798 describe its re-roofing and window glazing. Map evidence indicates that between 1760 and 1814 the front, north wall of the bawn and the north-west flanking tower were demolished and the area re-landscaped as gardens. The Vintners Company ended its involvement with Ulster, selling off its remaining properties, in the early nineteenth century. The bawn remained in private ownership and occupied until 1984. It then stood empty, in a semi-derelict condition until 1988, when the NIEA acquired it as a State Care monument.

As well as a comprehensive architectural survey of the standing buildings, one of the first tasks in preparing the site for conservation and presentation was to establish what survived of the Vintners Company's early seventeenth-century buildings. Three of the four walls of the square bawn enclosure, albeit not in their original condition, could be deduced from modern building lines, while the surviving round flanking tower clearly retained original brick fabric (Plate vi). But of Sir Baptist Jones' two houses, no trace was visible. It was clear from Raven's 1622 picture-map that the site of Jones' home, the 'manner house', lay beneath the still-standing Georgian house, while the site of the second house, occupied in the 1620s by his daughter Charity and her husband, lay on open ground on the western side of the bawn interior.

Small-scale trenching in 1989 established that a metre of mixed garden soils had accumulated over the remains of this second house, and a mechanical digger was brought in to clear it. Sir Thomas Phillips had described in his report of 1622 "one house of Brick...54 foot long, 26 foot broad, one storie high". The archaeologists discovered that the southern end of the house had survived at foundation level (Plate 5.7), while garden terracing had erased the northern end.

Plate 5.7 The stone foundations of the house within the bawn at Bellaghy. Note the curving line of boulders which gave the first clue to the presence of the underlying rath (NIEA).

Although the historical accounts and the surviving remains agreed in showing that the house had been built of hand-made brick, excavation found that its foundations were of small stone boulders, functioning as damp proofing. In the centre of the house stood the foundations of a large H-plan chimney base, with two back-to-back hearths of small pitched cobbles, edged by vertically-bedded slates. The chimney divided the house into two rooms, north and south, and the plans of such early seventeenth-century 'English' houses suggest that the space to the east, between the chimney and the front wall, functioned as a lobby entered via the front door.

The southern room had been floored with large cobbles. There was no evidence of cobbling in the northern room, and it was probably floored with timber planks. This suggests that, on entering the house's lobby, turning left took you into the kitchen, while turning right took you into the parlour, or living room. While Phillips described the house as single storey, Raven's drawing suggests first-floor dormer windows, and thus bedrooms in the roof space. Access to these may have been by a steep or spiral staircase on the western side of the central chimneystack.

On acquiring the site, one of the main conservation problems was the alarming outward lean of the western bawn wall. This was clearly not a recent phenomenon, as the wall had been clad in stone, probably in the eighteenth century, to lend it structural stability. Identifying the root cause of this problem, so as to rectify it at its source, was aided by three observations made during the house's excavation. One was a large fracture that could be observed in the chimneystack. A second was that the kitchen's cobbled floor had markedly subsided to the west. The third (and ultimately the vital clue) was a line of large boulders found within the kitchen cobbles (Plate 5.7). These were so distinctive that they could not have been part of the early seventeenth-century floor, and in fact, pre-dated it.

Plate 5.8 The trench excavated to confirm the presence of the rath ditch, with its V-shaped profile (NIEA).

It is an archaeological truism that 'a good site is a good site'; a site chosen in one era for its favourable topography will be chosen again in a later era for the same reasons. Early seventeenth-century commentaries record that a number of Ulster Plantation bawns were deliberately built on 'Danish forts' (Early Medieval period raths) for precisely this reason. Although there was no such historical evidence at Bellaghy, it appeared likely that Sir Baptist Jones had built his bawn and its houses on top of a rath. Targeted excavations rapidly revealed a V-shaped ditch (Plate 5.8), surviving to a depth of 1.5m, which had defined the rath perimeter. The boulders beneath the kitchen floor were part of a revetment which had supported an interior earthen bank. The chimneystack fracture, the kitchen floor's subsidence and the western bawn wall's lean were all the result of Jones' ignorance of, or indifference to, the infilled rath ditch beneath his feet. He had built on soft ground.

North of this house, hopes of finding traces of the long-demolished flanking tower were slight. Fortunately, the brick-lined socket of the timber door-sill of the tower survived, and it was possible (on the basis that this structure was a mirror of the surviving tower), to project its original ground plan.

A square, brick tower stands in the south-west corner of the bawn, adjacent to the 'gun platform'. Neither correlated accurately with the early seventeenth-century accounts, and excavation established that the surviving platform was an enlarged, eighteenth-century version of its predecessor, encapsulating the damaged original within it. Interestingly, the rampart had been riven by a massive fissure, further evidence of subsidence caused by the underlying Early Medieval period ditch. The early seventeenth-century platform appears to have been deliberately razed, and a 1639 French coin found within the demolition rubble hints that this took place during the 1641 hostilities. The later platform sealed the settings for sandstone steps leading up to the original corner tower, cobbling of the bawn interior, and a brick-lined drain for surface water to drain out through the bawn wall. The tower proved to be of eighteenth-century construction, reusing early brick.

Later excavations, inside the Georgian house, in advance of its conservation, found further evidence of the Early Medieval period rath, including the ditch, stake-hole patterns suggestive of houses, and Souterrain Ware. Unfortunately, evidence of Sir Baptist Jones' 'manner house' was scant.

Chapter 6
Afterlife

Chapter 6: Afterlife

Introduction

The subject of death is compelling not least to archaeologists, as skeletal remains provide tangible relics of the people who once inhabited and manipulated the landscape we have inherited. The ways in which people disposed of their dead has changed over the millennia with prehistoric megaliths and Christian cemeteries probably being the most widely recognised traditions in Ireland. The archaeological investigation of these and other mortuary practices has the potential not only for the recovery of the physical remains of our predecessors, but also for revealing information on cultural responses to death, and life, and on the social organisation of different communities. Indeed, much of our understanding of pre-Christian, pagan populations derives from burials and burial monuments.

There is a bias in the archaeological record towards those periods that distinguished their dead monumentally in stone, in particular during the prehistoric period, with megaliths, stone cists and barrows. Only a tiny minority of the population would, however, have been accorded special burial in these tomb types. For the majority, burial practices must have prevailed which are more elusive archaeologically although occasionally, fortuitous discoveries provide a glimpse of other more modest and ephemeral burials.

Human remains and other evidence for burials are extremely rare in the Irish Mesolithic and none have been found to date in Northern Ireland. The limited evidence at this time consists of a small number of disarticulated skeletal remains, mostly recovered from caves that have been radiocarbon dated to the Mesolithic, and just one true burial – two cremation pits from County Limerick – is known.

The succeeding Neolithic is probably best known for its burial monuments, the megalithic tombs. Essentially these are above-ground burial chambers, built of large stone slabs and covered with earth or small stones forming a cairn. Megaliths come in a wide variety of forms with different distribution patterns and periods of use. The megalithic burial tradition also continues into the Early Bronze Age with the erection of wedge tombs. Although they served as tombs, the ritual use and significance of these monuments is indicated by the presence of passages, courts and sometimes megalithic art. Many are also aligned with astronomical events such as the rising or setting of the sun on the solstices. Excavations have uncovered hearths, pits and deposits of animal bones, pottery or other material remains at many of these sites (as at Newtownstewart and Ballintaggart, discussed in this chapter) suggesting that some form of burial feast or sacrificial rites may also have taken place. All of these different aspects indicate that the monuments had a greater role than just as repositories for the remains of the dead. Perhaps we should not view these as simply tombs but more as venues where multiple rituals were carried out.

The bones that were presumably originally deposited in megaliths, both cremations and inhumations, only rarely survive. Analysis of the few surviving skeletal assemblages has suggested that the Neolithic processed their dead and that they selected only certain parts of the body for interment. This implies physical dismemberment of some form either after excarnation, as has been suggested may have taken place at Ballynahatty (see Chapter 2), or, the deliberate skinning and dissection of the dead which has been recorded at the unusual Neolithic complex at Millin Bay in County Down. The majority of these megalithic skeletal deposits also comprise the remains of many people indicating that the tombs acted as a communal repository for bones.

The primary difference that distinguishes the treatment of the dead in the Neolithic from the succeeding Bronze Age and Iron Age, is a move from communal to individual burial. However, the practice of occasional multiple and double burials, often of an adult and child (see Newtownstewart, discussed in this chapter), continues. There was a remarkable variety of funeral practices in the Bronze Age. The rites included inhumations, typically in a crouched or flexed position, and cremation burials which may be in, under or accompanied by pottery vessels, in cists or pits. These cists are found both singly, as at Newtownstewart and in cemeteries, as at Ballintaggart. The emptied cists at the centre of the Copney stone circles (see Chapter 2) were also presumably for burials forming a Bronze Age cemetery of sorts. Burials are also often placed within cairns and barrows, a tradition that continues into the Iron Age. In the Bronze Age grave goods are often found, most notably different types of pots (see Newtownstewart and Ballintaggart in this chapter). Some of the pots were termed 'Food Vessels' by antiquarians because it was believed that they may have held offerings of food for the dead in the afterlife. If this suggestion is true, it would indicate people's belief in a life after death. A substantial proportion of all prehistoric burials, including those from the Neolithic, Bronze Age and Iron Age are cremations (see Newtownstewart and Ballintaggart in this chapter, and Ballynahatty in Chapter 2), and it is not until nearly two millennia later, in the nineteenth century, that this custom of cremation is again practised in Ireland.

At the start of the first millennium AD, influences from the Roman world filtered through to Ireland and the practice of extended inhumation burial was widely adopted. Conversion of the Irish population to Christianity took several centuries and it wasn't until the fifth century AD that it achieved broad acceptance while burials in churchyard cemeteries did not become the norm until the eighth and ninth centuries. Early Christian burials were placed in unprotected dug graves or slab-lined lintel graves. The bodies they contained were laid in an extended supine position, orientated east-west and often with their legs and feet found very close together indicating that the body was wrapped in a shroud. As many of these early Christian cemeteries have continued in use, few graveyards have been investigated, though recent exceptions include Solar and Armoy, both in County Antrim (see below in this chapter).

Another phenomenon that arose in conjunction with the increasing power and popularity, and propagandist intentions, of the early Church was the cult of relics. Bones and associated material accessories of founder saints, such as bells and pastoral staffs ('the flying crozier of Mo-choí of Nendrum' for example), were venerated as relics while the saints' burial places were a central focus of their cults. Many cemeteries had stone-built house-shaped shrines erected above the grave of the revered person, sometimes with openings so the devout could reach in and touch them. Relics were also housed in portable reliquaries such as the miniature seventh-century Clonmore shrine recently recovered, piecemeal, from the River Blackwater in County Armagh (see Chapter 3) and the twelfth-century Drumadoon bell shrine (see Chapter 1). This fashion for curating skeletal remains and objects is also suggested for a much earlier period as represented by the cremated remains discovered in the Newtownstewart cist, discussed in this chapter. This highlights the possibility of much greater nuances and subtleties in former attitudes to death and burial rites than we have yet had evidence to consider in Ireland or that are archaeologically detectable.

An unusual prehistoric grave at Newtownstewart Castle, County Tyrone

Ruairí Ó Baoill

Archaeological investigations took place at Newtownstewart Castle, County Tyrone in 1999 in tandem with conservation work on the castle walls with the view to opening the monument to the public. It was hoped that the excavation would help to work out the internal layout of the ruined

Plate 6.1 The Early Bronze Age cist in front of Newtownstewart Castle (NIEA).

seventeenth-century Plantation castle, so it came as a big surprise when a 4,000-year-old grave was found on the site. The grave, a segmented cist, took the form of a rectangular stone box, sub-divided into two compartments, and dates from the Irish Early Bronze Age.

The survival of this ancient tomb was remarkable. The area immediately in front of the castle near where the cist was discovered had been built over by twentieth-century structures, the foundations of which could easily have destroyed the grave. The capstone forming the lid of the cist was found just below the modern ground surface and was partially covered in concrete. The stone was initially thought to be part of an earlier street surface pre-dating modern Townhall Street. When the stone was removed, in the glare of television lights, the full significance of the discovery was revealed (Plates 6.1 and 6.2). The cist was roughly rectangular in shape, oriented north-south, and until that moment, had lain undisturbed. It was constructed of nine stones: two long side slabs, two end slabs, a central upright slab separating the cist into the two unequal sized compartments (called Chambers A and B), three flat basal slabs and the capstone. In each of the chambers a pile of cremated human bone and a highly decorated clay pot were found (Plates 6.3 and 6.4). The Chamber A cremation also contained a burnt flint arrowhead.

The undecorated capstone was roughly 1.5m long, 1m wide and 0.2m thick and would have required considerable manpower to lift into place. In prehistoric times only this stone would have been visible above ground and it was supported by the upright slabs of the cist. The stone cist was constructed within a pit and the space between the wall of the pit and the cist was filled with small stones. The capstone was then laid on top and sealed the tomb.

Examination of the cremated bone from the grave was conducted by Eileen Murphy of Queen's University, Belfast. In Chamber A, the larger of the two, roughly a third of the bone fragments were identifiable and comprised skull, axial and limb fragments. It was concluded that the remains represented a complete or near-complete skeleton of a 12–15-year-old adolescent. It was not

Plate 6.2 The pots and cremated human bone in the Newtownstewart cist – open for all to see after more than 4,000 years (NIEA).

Plate 6.3 The two bipartite Early Bronze Age bowls from the Newtownstewart cist (NIEA).

Plate 6.4 Basal view of the two bowls (NIEA).

possible to determine the sex of the individual. In Chamber B, roughly half of the bone fragments were also identifiable as skull, axial and limb fragments. These bones were of a woman who had died in her 40s or 50s and who had suffered from tooth loss and had had problems with her joints.

The bone fragments recovered from Newtownstewart cist displayed marked uniformity in their colour, and the vast majority of fragments were pale grey or white suggesting that these individuals had been cremated at temperatures of between 645° C and 1200° C (human cremation processes are discussed further by Murphy and Heaney later in this chapter).

The arrowhead found with the cremated bones of the adolescent was a hollow-based type which is rare compared with the barbed and tanged types more common from Bronze Age sites in Ulster. The Newtownstewart arrowhead, although completely burnt, was relatively intact and finely made. One possible explanation as to why it survived so well may have been that it was lodged inside the cremated individual, although no identifiable impact damage (due to contact with bone) was observed on the tip of the projectile. Experimental tests on the burning of flint flakes carried out at Queen's University, Belfast by Barrie Hartwell have suggested that temperatures in excess of 900° C are required to completely calcine or burn flint specimens. This provides additional evidence for the heat of the cremation pyres.

Given the size of the pyre necessary to burn a human body it would be expected that large quantities of charcoal and ash should be found with the cremated remains. A number of fragments of charcoal and of a grey-white ash-like substance were recovered from both of the Newtownstewart cremation deposits but not a substantial amount, suggesting that after cremation the human bone was deliberately separated from the pyre debris. The picture that emerges is of a religious ceremony, with the members of a settlement attending, or at least being able to witness from a distance, what must have been considerable funeral pyres. After the fires had died down, the cremated bone would have been retrieved and deposited, along with the pots, within the cist. Food or drink to sustain the dead in the afterlife may also have been placed in the tomb, perhaps in the accompanying vessels. The final act, of erecting the large capstone, must have been a communal act.

It would seem reasonable to speculate that the people interred within the two chambers of the cist were related and this bond may be mirrored in the similarity of decoration on the two bowls. It is also likely that they were of relatively high status to afford such a significant burial. The fact that the juvenile was accorded equal status as the adult female would also suggest that gender and age were not as important as the bonds of kinship. It is possible that the Newtownstewart cist represents one example from what may originally have been a larger cemetery. The area available for archaeological investigation around the castle was extremely limited, nevertheless, no other graves were found, nor any evidence of a bank, ditch or post-holes that might have marked out the perimeter of such a cemetery.

The radiocarbon dates returned for samples of the bone raise some interesting questions. There was a 95% probability that the date range for the sample from Chamber A (the juvenile) fell between 2475 and 2212 BC, while the sample from Chamber B (the adult female) fell between 2195 and 1951 BC. As there is no overlap in the dates, this indicates that the people died at different times and it raises the possibility that the cremations were not carried out contemporaneously. The excavation of the cist showed, however, that the interment of the bones was a single episode while the close similarity in the decoration of the two pots would suggest that they were made around the same time if not by the same person. The question of the careful curation of remains, over at least one if not several generations, before their deposition in the cist must be considered. This possibility of curation questions our archaeological knowledge of prehistoric burial practices and highlights the possibility of much greater complexities in the death rites that were formerly practised than we have yet had evidence to consider in Ireland. It also raises the intriguing issue of the practicalities of such a ritual – where were the remains kept over the intervening years? Although there is no direct evidence from Newtownstewart, recent evidence from Bronze Age sites in Scotland suggests that mummification of human remains might have been one of the processes of curation. The other possibility is that the cremated remains of the juvenile were curated in some way.

Numerous explanations for the later re-interment of the juvenile can be suggested. One possibility is that a change in funeral rites may have occurred with the reburial of someone using the newly adopted custom. Another explanation might be that there was a population movement, due to warfare or in the quest for better resources, with the removal of the remains of important people to the new location, possibly even as a symbolic founding gesture. The location of the burial seems also to be significant as it overlooks an important fording point at the junction of the Strule and Owenvarra Rivers.

Segmented cists are rare, amounting to perhaps only 1% or 2% of known Irish Bronze Age graves. The discovery of the well preserved cist of this type at Newtownstewart in such unexpected circumstances and yielding the hollow-based arrowhead, decorated pots and cremated remains of a possibly curated individual marks it as highly significant.

Further reading

Ó Baoill, R. 2005 'Excavation of a segmented Bronze Age cist at Newtownstewart, County Tyrone', *Ulster Journal of Archaeology* 64, 26–42.

A Middle to Late Bronze Age cemetery at Ballintaggart, Loughbrickland, County Down

Eileen Murphy and Lianne Heaney

In March 2004 Northern Archaeological Consultancy Ltd, undertook a series of excavations along the A1 road between Loughbrickland and Beech Hill, County Down, prior to the broadening of the carriageway. The work uncovered a substantial number of sites, including three Early Neolithic houses (Plate iv), a burnt mound and numerous Bronze Age burials, indicating the importance of this area for prehistoric people over a considerable period of time. This section focuses on the latter, a Middle to Late Bronze Age cemetery discovered at Ballintaggart.

Plate 6.5 General site photo of Ballintaggart, looking south-east, showing the Bronze Age barrow cemetery in the foreground with the old and new Newry-Belfast roads in the background (NIEA).

Plate 6.6 Ring-ditches at Ballintaggart under excavation (NIEA).

Eight circular ring-ditches, ranging from less than 2m to over 6m in diameter were uncovered across an area of 900m^2 (Plates 6.5 and 6.6). Deposits of cremated human remains were found in pits in the central enclosed area of each. It is probable that these burials were covered by a low mound or barrow made with the soil excavated from the enclosing ditches, but these did not survive due to intensive ploughing in recent years. Two four-poster structures, one of which was enclosed by a ring-ditch, were also found. These structures, as their name would suggest, comprised four post-holes which would have held timber posts and they surrounded a central cremation burial in a pit. The structures are an unusual finding for Ireland and are more commonly associated with Bronze Age Scotland. Radiocarbon dating has indicated that the cemetery at Ballintaggart was used from the Middle into the Late Bronze Age spanning at most some 800 years, from 1640 BC to 790 BC.

Several features in the cemetery appeared to align with each other as well as with various landscape features around them. Four of the ring-ditches formed a row, some 20m long, and the dating evidence indicates that three of these were broadly contemporary. This line of ring-ditches was orientated towards a dip in the hillside to the north-west, and it is feasible that the row had been deliberately aligned upon the sunset of the summer solstice. A second group of features, two of the ring-ditches and one of the four-posters were equally spaced from one another and seemed to align on an earthwork feature – Water Hill Fort – a large unexcavated barrow on Brickland Hill to the north-east.

The ring-ditch burials, both multiple and single, were all cremations though the cremated remains were deposited in a variety of ways. A number of the cremations had been deposited in large coarse, flat-bottomed urns set into pits, encircled by the ring-ditches, while the burial of an adult female recovered from one of the later sites had been laid within a Vase Food Vessel (Plate 6.7). One of the burials had been placed within a stone-lined cist and in others the cremated bones had been placed directly in pits in the ground.

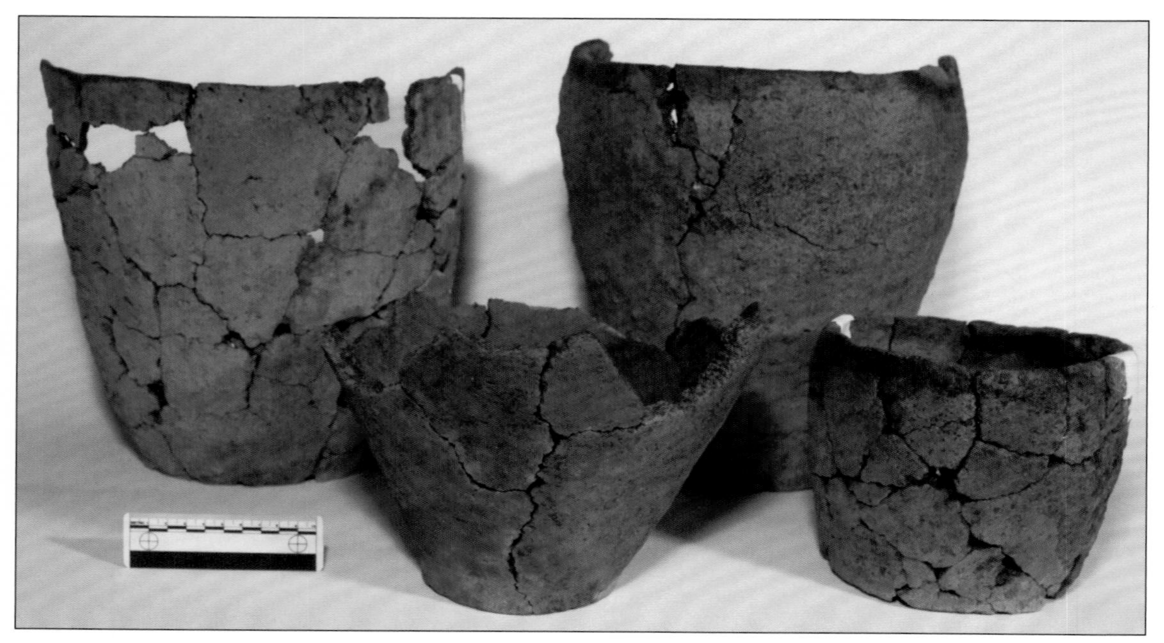

Plate 6.7 Bronze Age vessels from Ballintaggart that contained cremations, following conservation (NAC Ltd).

In total, 15 individuals were represented in the 9 excavated burial sites and these comprised 10 adults and 5 children. The children were represented by a newborn infant, a 3–6-year-old child and three older children (8–18 years) while the adults included four females and three males. A small number of palaeopathological lesions were apparent; an 8–14-year-old child and an adult female both displayed cribra orbitalia. This is a sieve-like lesion in the roof of the eye socket and is widely accepted as being indicative of childhood iron deficiency anaemia which can be caused by blood loss through excessive bleeding or parasitic infestation, diarrhoea or nutritional deficiencies. Some five adults displayed degenerative joint changes of their spine and these lesions, on the vertebrae or rib heads, are probably due to everyday wear and tear on the joints and to the ageing process. Evidence of a stressed muscle attachment was visible on a fragment of knee cap from an adult male. The lesion had probably arisen as a consequence of stress and strain having been placed on part of a tendon of the joint. A second adult male recovered from the same burial displayed evidence for the ante-mortem loss of at least five mandibular teeth. Three root tips displayed a bulbous appearance and it is considered possible that the individual had been suffering from a chronic, low grade dental infection.

In terms of burial practice it is clear that there was a huge variety. Only three sites had been used for the burial of single individuals – an adult, a teenager and an adult female. During the excavation of two of the ring-ditches and one of the four-poster structures it was suspected that the central areas had been reused for later burials and osteological analysis confirmed this to have been the case. As yet, we are uncertain as to the length of time that would have elapsed between the different insertions and a number of questions remain to be answered. Are we seeing the deliberate reuse of a grave to enable, for example, family members to be buried together? Alternatively, is this simply the opportunistic reuse of a burial site at a later date?

The cremation deposit recovered from one of the ring-ditches contained the remains of a 25–45-year-old female, a 3–6-year-old child and a newborn infant. It is possible to speculate that this group may represent a mother and her children who had died during a single event. Further support for this theory can be found in the appearance of the cremated bone. The cremation process requires heat, oxygen and time for it to be successful, and if any of these variables are lacking it may be incomplete. The colour of cremated bone reflects the amount of oxidisation the organic components of the bone have undergone, and is partly dependent on temperature. When bones are subjected to increasingly higher temperatures they change from black, through various shades of grey, to white. Experimental studies on modern animal bones have indicated that bone changes to a white or pale yellow colour at temperatures of between 645° C and 1200° C, while black and grey discoloration generally occurs at temperatures of between 285° C and 525° C.

The remains recovered from most of the burials at Ballintaggart were a uniform white/pale grey colour thereby indicating that the cremated individuals had been burned on efficient pyres. The fragments derived from the three individuals (possibly from the same family – female, child and infant) buried in the same ring-ditch, however, were a uniform dark brown colour with white tinges, and it would appear probable that all three had been burned at a temperature less than 285° C. This may have been a deliberate act or perhaps it was simply the case that weather conditions on the day were not conducive to the creation of high temperatures. Alternatively, one might speculate that the multiple burials may be an indication that a calamitous event, such as disease or warfare, had struck the group. Such an event – which in this case might have wiped out most of a family – may have meant that it was only possible to invest limited resources in the creation of this particular pyre.

It is also possible to gain insights relating to adult burial practice by looking at the weight of each deposit and the size of its fragments. The weight of a cremated adult male ranges from approximately 1500g to 3600g, while females have a weight range of around 950g to 2300g. Of the 10 adults represented in the Ballintaggart burials only 3 had quantities of bone close to these expected values. In contrast, the remaining seven adults were represented by much smaller quantities of bone. It is possible that this situation arose, in some cases, because initial burials were disturbed by later insertions, although the possibility that a number of the burials could represent token, rather than complete deposits, should also be entertained.

The process of cremation does not necessarily produce fragments of small size. In fact, it seems to be the case that where deposits largely comprise fragments less than 10mm in size they have been deliberately pulverised prior to deposition. Only two of the burials produced substantial proportions of fragments in excess of 10mm in size suggesting that most of the adult remains had been subject to some form of pulverisation prior to their deposition.

The burial practices represented at Ballintaggart – token cremation deposits accompanied by coarse ware pots, absence of individualising grave goods, variety of funerary monuments and multiple burials in a 'cemetery' – are all characteristic of later Middle and Late Bronze Age burial practices. It is often thought that the lack of high status grave goods accompanying the dead in the latter half of the Bronze Age is representative of an egalitarian society. A degree of caution should, however, be exercised when considering this issue. At Ballintaggart it is clear that a range of elaborate funerary rituals would have taken place prior to interment. Time and energy would have been invested in the construction and management of an efficient funerary pyre as well as, in at least some cases, the selection of bone elements and their pulverisation. Effort would also have been needed to construct the ring-ditch and barrow. It has been suggested that high status members of society were affirming their position through these complicated funerary ceremonies.

The nature of these funerary monuments may also indicate a continued desire to make burials focal points on the landscape, perhaps for territorial reasons, as had been the case with the megalithic tombs of the Neolithic and Early Bronze Age periods. If we accept this interpretation, then we can suggest the individuals buried at Ballintaggart may have been among the elite of society. It would therefore seem to be the case that all individuals – from the youngest baby through to adult males and females – could potentially have held high status within Middle and Late Bronze Age society.

Further reading

Chapple, R.M., Dunlop, C., Gilmore, S. and Heaney, L. 2009 *Archaeological investigations along the A1 dualling scheme, Loughbrickland to Beech Hill, Co. Down, N. Ireland (2005)* (BAR British Series 479). Oxford: Archaeopress.

Solar studies – an Early Medieval cemetery investigated

Declan Hurl

The townland of Solar lies on the eastern slope of Black Hill, midway between the villages of Ballygally and Glenarm on the east Antrim coast. Foundations of the Early Medieval stone-built church of Solar (14.5m by 6m) were discernible in mid-Victorian times, as recorded by the Reverend William Reeves, although no upstanding remnants of this building are currently visible. The field wall running adjacent to the site was, however, allegedly built with stone from the church, which might explain its disappearance over recent decades. This ecclesiastical site is known for the 'Bell of Solar', an Early Medieval iron hand-bell found in the early twentieth century and now held in the Ulster Museum. It was also the centre of a small Late Medieval parish of the

Plate 6.8 Excavation trenches at Solar with Black Hill in the distance (NIEA).

Plate 6.9 One of the stone-lined graves found quite close to the site of the early church (NIEA).

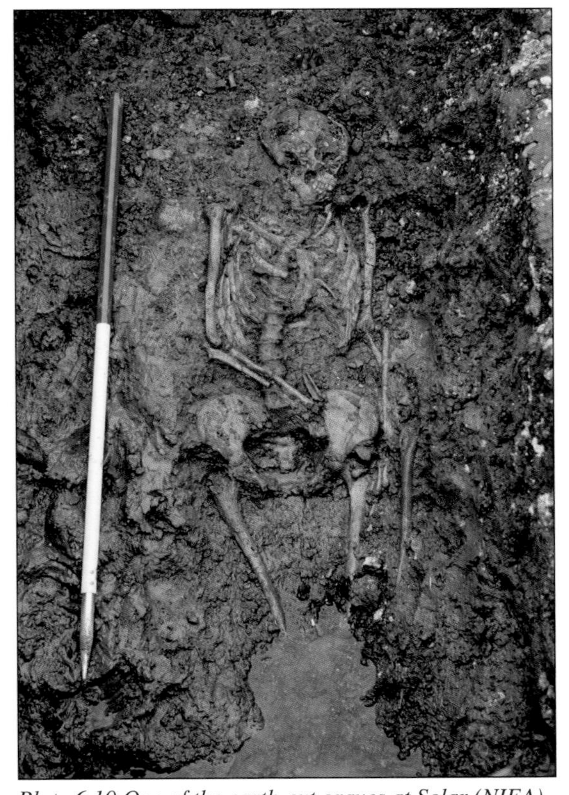

Plate 6.10 One of the earth-cut graves at Solar (NIEA).

same name. A sandstone font or stoup, reportedly from the church site and kept at a farm nearby, probably belongs to this later period of use. Little other information or documentation survives on the church site.

In 1993 the farmer who owned the land sought to dig a silage pit in a field close to the old church. However, as this was within the scheduled area of the monument, archaeological excavation was required to determine whether any significant archaeological features survived.

The test trenches (Plate 6.8) revealed that the field contained a cemetery associated with the Early Medieval church. In total there were 123 individuals represented by the skeletal remains uncovered. These included the articulated remains of 63 adults (including 24 males and 35 females) and 14 juveniles. There were a further 35 adults (including 7 males and 10 females) and 11 juveniles represented by the disarticulated remains.

Nine graves contained stone-lined burials in the part of the field nearest to the early church (Plate 6.9). All of the nine were of adult males and dated from the seventh or eighth century, as determined by radiocarbon analysis. The other burials were in plain earth-cut graves, many of which were covered by spreads of chalk and flint nodules (Plates 6.10 and 6.11). White stones, typically quartz, are common on graves in Early Medieval ecclesiastical sites across Britain and Ireland and indeed this practice continues in some places up to the present day. The precise origin of the custom is uncertain although white has traditionally been the Christian colour of religious life and purity and there are many references to its significance in the Bible and other ecclesiastical writings.

Plate 6.11 One of the earth-cut graves at Solar (NIEA).

Plate 6.12 One of the three crouched burials excavated at Solar (NIEA).

The stone-lined burials closest to the church represent the earliest phase of the cemetery which expanded outwards to the south and east over subsequent decades and centuries of use, with the latest burial dated to the late tenth to early thirteenth century. Women and children were also found to be more frequently buried furthest from the church. The limits of the cemetery appeared to be marked by a terrace which was dug in a rough arc around 25m from the church site. The early stone-lined burials were also contained within this terraced area although the excavation demonstrated that some of these overlay an earlier ditch. No dating evidence was recovered from this ditch but it is possible that it was also Early Medieval in date and associated with an earlier phase of development of the ecclesiastical site.

The majority of the skeletons were laid in an extended, supine position orientated approximately east-west with their heads to the west. Three crouched burials were also found, two laid on their right sides and one on its left (Plate 6.12), and one of which was orientated north-south. Whether this latter deviation denoted a less than reverential approach to the deceased by the burial party is impossible to determine, especially over one thousand years on, but it must be a suspicion. Another unusual burial was that of a young woman. Her head had been set on her chest, though there were no obvious signs of decapitation, and she was pregnant. Again, it is impossible to say whether those two details were connected.

Few artefacts were recovered in the 1993 investigations, save for some sherds of Souterrain Ware, and a few pieces of Saintonge Ware, a fine glazed French pottery brought in by the Anglo-Normans. There was, however, a bronze pennanular brooch dating to the late eighth or early ninth century, found near one of the burials towards the centre of the excavation site. Topsoil stripping across the site in 1990 was much more prolific in terms of finds and revealed a dense scatter of artefacts to the south-west of the church site. These included hundreds of sherds of Souterrain Ware, Medieval Ulster coarse pottery and Late Medieval glazed wares especially in the vicinity of the church, as well as a rotary quern stone and a socketed iron spearhead. No apparent structural features were noted at that time.

Once the archaeological relevance of the field was revealed, the plan to dig the silage pit was abandoned. A few years later the *Historic Monuments and Archaeological Objects (NI) Order, 1995* extended further protection to Solar and, because of this, the site cannot be further disturbed without official permission.

Further reading

Hurl, D.P. 2002 'The excavation of an Early Christian cemetery at Solar, County Antrim, 1993', *Ulster Journal of Archaeology* 61, 37–82.

Human remains from St Patrick's Church, Armoy, County Antrim

Eileen Murphy

In spring 1997 excavations took place, in advance of major refurbishment, at St Patrick's Church of Ireland church in Armoy, County Antrim, under the direction of Declan Hurl of the NIEA. The site of the church has Early Medieval associations being linked to St Olcan, and is located beside the stump of a round tower. The present church, orientated east-west, was built in 1820 and then extended in 1869. It was constructed on the site of the Medieval church, which appears to have been orientated north-south, and is situated at the eastern end of the original part of the modern church. In the *Taxation of Pope Nicholas* of 1306 'Ecclesia de Ethirmoy' was valued at £4 11s. 8d.

Plate 6.13 Interior of St Patrick's Church, Armoy during excavation (NIEA).

In the *Ulster Visitation* book of 1622, however, the Medieval church was described as being 'unrepayred', suggesting that it had become abandoned or had fallen into ruin. The exact date when the Medieval church fell into decline is not known.

During the excavation in the church's interior (Plate 6.13) four main trenches were opened – two at the eastern end of the church, near the altar, and two at the western end, near the main doorway. At a depth of approximately one metre, large quantities of disarticulated human remains were uncovered which directly overlay the remains of some 56 articulated skeletons. Radiocarbon dating of a number of the individuals indicated that they ranged in date from the fifteenth century up until as late as the first half of the twentieth century.

Many of the skeletons had been truncated by later burials but some were in a very good state of preservation. In a number of cases it was possible to ascertain that the bodies had been buried within wooden coffins as traces of wood and nails had survived. All the bodies were orientated east-west as would be expected for Christian burials. It is probable that most individuals would have been buried shortly after death but this may not have been the case for one man whose cranium was found to contain numerous insect pupa cases. Analysis of the pupae by Robert Nash of the Ulster Museum ascertained that they belonged to the genus *Ofyra*. These are carnivorous insects who feed off the bugs which initially invade a newly dead corpse. As such, it is probable that, for whatever reason, burial of the body had not taken place for at least one month after death.

The remains of men, women and children were present and many of the children were found to have died at less than two years of age – a typical trend for a pre-industrial population. The adult males had an average stature of around 1.67m (5'6"), while that of females was 1.55m (5'1"). These values suggest the Medieval people buried at St Patrick's were generally shorter in height than the modern Irish population. Many of the skeletons displayed evidence of disease and poor health. Some nine individuals displayed signs of having suffered from active infections when they died. In most cases these infections would have been caused by a variety of soil and airborne bacteria, including *staphylococci* and *streptococci*. Two teenagers displayed particularly nasty infections which had affected their lower leg bones. In each case the affected bone was swollen and at least one abscess cavity, which would have enabled the escape of pus from the centre of the bone, was visible. Possible evidence for a large skin ulcer was evident in the lower leg bone of an adult male (Plate 6.14). In the pre-antibiotic era, infection would have been one of the main causes of death and this certainly seems to have been the case for some of the people buried at St Patrick's Church.

Two individuals may have suffered from tuberculosis, and a definite case of leprosy was identified. A radiocarbon date derived from the leprosy sufferer provided a date range of between the mid fifteenth and mid seventeenth century AD, and it is probably one of the oldest individuals in the assemblage. This case was of particular interest since it is, as yet, the only definite instance of this horrendous disease to have been identified in the archaeological record for Ireland. Only the feet were preserved but the severity of the bone changes suggest that the unfortunate individual would have suffered from the most severe form of the disease (lepromatous leprosy) (Plate 6.15). He or she may well have had the characteristic facial changes of leprosy, with a collapsed bridge of the nose, missing upper front teeth, loss of eyebrows, swollen upper eyelids, and skin nodules. It is possible that the disease had progressed to a stage were the person was also hoarse and blind. It is likely that the hands would have had stumps for fingers, as was certainly the case with regard to the toes, while the feet and lower legs would probably have been ulcerated.

Other lesions present in the Armoy remains included degenerative joint disease and Schmorl's nodes which probably attest to the strenuous physical lifestyles of the individuals. It is notable

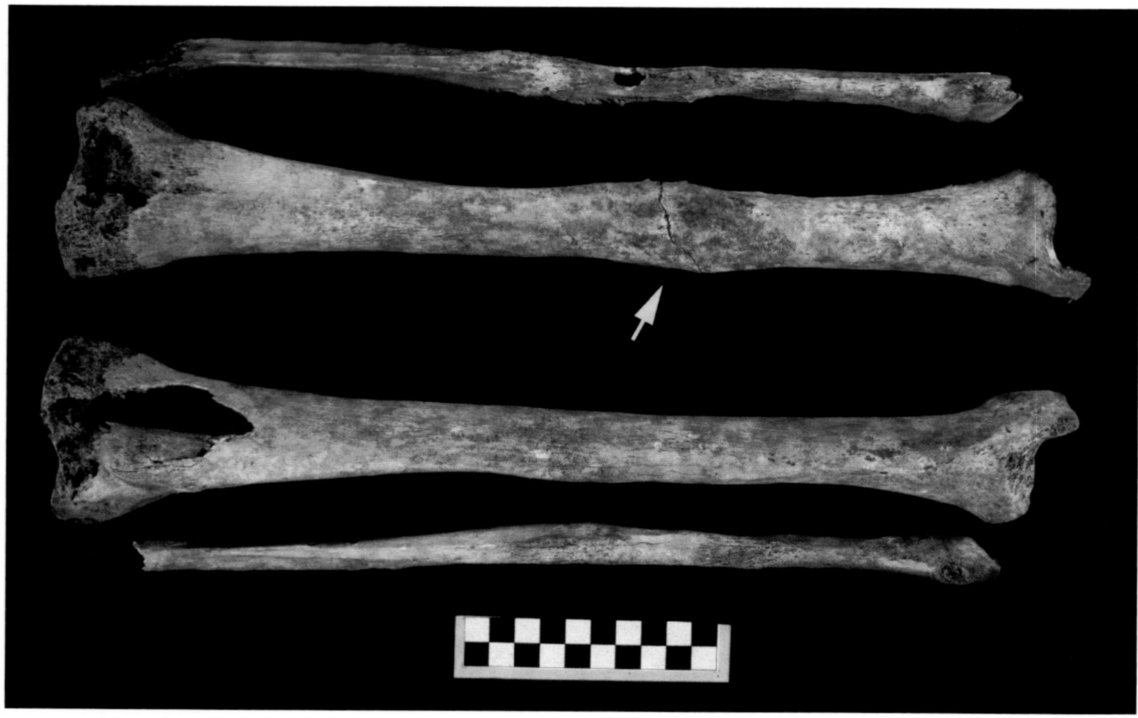

Plate 6.14 Possible evidence for an overlying skin ulcer in the left tibia of an adult male from Armoy (NIEA).

that no signs of trauma were present; this is strange since it is usually the case that the occasional fractured bone would be encountered in a population group of this size. A number of individuals displayed cribra orbitalia, characteristic of iron deficiency anaemia, while some displayed dental enamel hypoplasia, a sign of childhood physiological stress. A variety of forms of dental disease was apparent, including ante-mortem tooth loss, periodontal disease, dental abscesses, caries and calculus deposits. The prevalence of caries among the adults (3.3%) was relatively low and more in keeping with findings from Irish Early Medieval period sites. Clinical studies have indicated that the most cariogenic foodstuffs are those which are sticky in texture, contain high levels of simple sugars and are consumed frequently throughout the day. It would seem to be the case, therefore, that the diet of the people buried at St Patrick's Church was not especially conducive to the development of caries.

The Church of Ireland permitted the excavation of the St Patrick's burials under the condition they would be reburied following their scientific study. When the refurbished church was opened on March 7th 1998 by the late Right Reverend James E. Moore, then Bishop of Connor, part of the ceremony involved the reburial of the remains in the church's graveyard. The bodies now rest in peace again but we are grateful for the insights that we were able to gain about these people from earlier times.

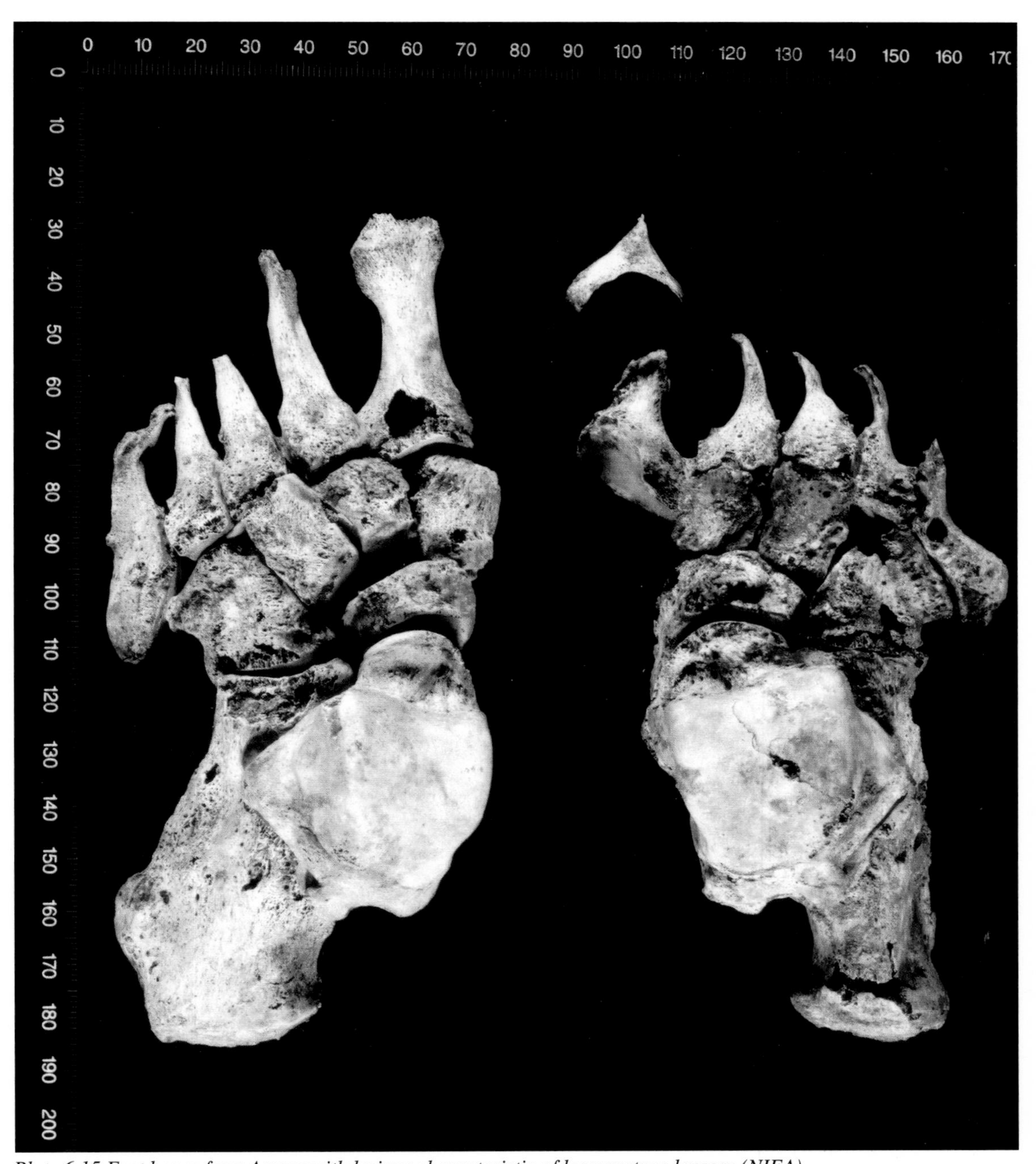

Plate 6.15 Feet bones from Armoy with lesions characteristic of lepromatous leprosy (NIEA).

Appendix 1

Abbreviations

AD	Anno Domini (in the year of our Lord). AD denotes years after the start of this epoch. There is no year zero; the year AD 1 immediately follows the year 1 BC.
ADS Ltd	Archaeological Development Services Limited
ACS Ltd	Archaeological Consultancy Services Limited
BC	Before Christ. BC denotes years before the start of this epoch.
CAF	Centre for Archaeological Fieldwork at Queen's University Belfast
CMA	Centre for Maritime Archaeology at University of Ulster
MBR	Monuments and Buildings Record
MRA	Maritime Register for County Antrim
NAC Ltd	Northern Archaeological Consultancy Limited
NIEA	Northern Ireland Environment Agency
QUB	Queen's University Belfast
SMR	Sites and Monuments Record (part of the MBR)
TSO	The Stationery Office
UJA	Ulster Journal of Archaeology
UM	Ulster Museum
UU	University of Ulster
WWT	Wildfowl and Wetlands Trust

Appendix 2

Keywords

The **Anglo-Normans** were the descendants of the Normans who ruled England following the Norman Conquest led by William of Normandy in 1066. Following the Battle of Hastings (1066), the invading Normans and their descendants formed a distinct population in Britain, as Normans controlled all of England, parts of Wales (the Cambro-Normans) and, after 1169, parts of eastern and southern Ireland.

The **annals** are yearly chronicles listing important incidents such as deaths and births of significant members of society, major battles and other noteworthy events, for example good and bad harvests. The earliest begin in the sixth and seventh centuries AD and some continue to the end of the sixteenth century. They were compiled in monasteries, though surviving annals, such as the *Annals of Ulster*, were transcribed at a much later date than the events to which they refer.

An **ard** is a primitive light plough that scratches the surface of the land rather than turning furrows.

Articulated complete or partial skeletons are those in which the skeletal parts are found in their correct anatomical, jointed, arrangement even when the ligaments and other tissues have decomposed. This indicates that the skeleton was not interred in a disjointed ('disarticulated') state and also that the articulated bones have not been disturbed at some time after their deposition.

A **barrel vault** is an architectural element within a building forming the roofing of a chamber (and support for the flooring above) using an arch or series of arches. The finished effect is that of a concave shape which is perhaps easiest to imagine by taking a barrel and cutting it in half lengthways and using one half to form a ceiling.

A **barrow** is a mound of earth or stones erected over a grave. Ring-barrows are circular earthworks with a central mound (barrow) surrounded by a ditch, and again, typically by a bank. The raised features, the barrow and bank, often do not survive leaving only the concentric ditch and central burial in which state the monument is often referred to as a ring-ditch. The majority of barrows/ring-barrows/ring-ditches date to the Bronze Age and Early Iron Age.

A **base-batter** is the thick base of a wall which slopes inwards towards the top.

A **bawn** is a fortified enclosure or courtyard. In Ireland this usually refers to part of the outwork of a tower-house or Plantation castle.

Calculus is a generic term for concretions occurring in the body. Calculus deposits on the teeth represent calcified dental plaque.

A **caliver** is a kind of light musket, weighing 9–10 pounds (4–4.5kg). The caliver was introduced during the sixteenth century as a light portable firearm that could be fired without a support.

Cambro-Norman (see Anglo-Norman)

Cariogenic foodstuffs are those which promote or cause tooth decay (caries).

Carinated Bowl pottery is the earliest type of pottery found in Ireland first appearing around the start of the Neolithic. The bowls in this style are simple, round-bottomed and undecorated and have distinctive ridged shoulders or carinations. They also typically have smoothed or burnished surfaces.

Carrowkeel Ware is a type of Late Neolithic pottery found primarily in megalithic tombs and other ritual structures. The forms comprise mainly round-bottomed bowls and hemispherical cups and are decorated with 'stab-and-drag' or impressed motifs. This ceramic type is named after Carrowkeel, a Neolithic passagetomb cemetery in the Bricklieve Mountains in south County Sligo.

A **cist** is a small stone-built box used for human burial, either cremations or inhumations. Cists are often found associated with other features, such as a cairn or barrow, and can occur singly or in groups of two or more together.

In brick-making a **clamp** is a carefully constructed stack of bricks and fuel used for firing bricks in the open air. Each clamp is only fired once and then dismantled to retrieve the useful bricks. Clamps represent the oldest method used for firing bricks but are wasteful of fuel and slow to fire.

Court tombs are a form of Neolithic megalithic tomb. They have a semicircular forecourt at the wider end of a relatively long cairn, which is usually trapezoidal in plan and supported by a kerb of stones along its sides. A burial gallery leads off the forecourt, subdivided into two or more chambers the side walls of which are built of orthostats supporting a roof of lintels or corbelling. The tombs have a northerly distribution in Ireland and excavations within a number of them have found both inhumation and cremation burials and artefacts including Neolithic pottery, stone beads and flint tools.

Crannogs are partially or wholly artificial islands of stone, timber and earth. They are typically circular or oval in plan and are generally found in small lakes. The majority that have been dated were constructed in the Early Medieval period, with a particular cluster in the seventh century AD. Prehistoric examples are also known, while some were occupied, reused or newly built, in the Late- and Post-Medieval periods.

A **creep** is a narrow or constricted part of a passage in a souterrain.

Crop marks occur due to the differential growth of a crop. One of the factors controlling the growth of plants is the condition of the soil. If there are differences in the soil conditions this will cause some plants to grow better than others resulting in taller growth, differential ripening or overall colour. A buried ditch for example, with a fill containing more organic matter and water than the ordinary cultivation soil, provides suitable conditions for the plants growing above. Conversely, buried walls generally provide less advantageous growing conditions. Differential growth will follow any features buried below the ground and therefore crop marks can reveal sub-surface archaeological features, with the patterns best seen from the air. By their nature crop marks are only visible seasonally and may not be visible at all except in exceptionally wet or dry years.

Crown glass is a form of hand-blown glass. It was first developed in the fourteenth century but wasn't widely produced until the late seventeenth century after which it dominated production and use as window glass, up until the mid nineteenth century. The process involves gathering molten glass on a blowpipe, and blowing a balloon shape. The blowpipe is then removed and a solid rod is attached and the glass is spun rapidly until a disc is formed. The outer portion beyond the central knob is then cut into panes.

A **crozier** is the pastoral staff or crook of a bishop or abbot.

Cullet refers to old, broken or waste glass which is melted down and recycled to make inferior glass.

Dendrochronology, or tree-ring dating, is a method of scientific dating based on the study of annual growth rings in trees and timbers.

Dental enamel hypoplasia is manifest as lines, grooves or pits on tooth enamel. These morphological changes arise when the tooth enamel is developing as a result of physiological stress during infancy and childhood illnesses or nutritional stress. It is also recorded on other mammals.

E-Ware is an imported wheel-thrown pottery from western France in circulation in the sixth, seventh and eighth centuries AD. The imported vessels may originally have contained luxury goods such as wine or oil.

An **emporium** is a place where goods are collected and traded.

The term **English Border ware** refers to a type of domestic pottery produced in the border region of the English counties of Hampshire and Surrey, primarily in the sixteenth and seventeenth centuries. It was made from white clays and is characterised by its yellow and green glazes.

Excarnation is the removal or stripping off of the fleshy parts of a body leaving only the bones. It may be precipitated through natural means, leaving a body exposed to rot and decay naturally and for animals to scavenge, or it may be purposefully undertaken by skinning, defleshing and butchering the corpse by hand.

Burnt mounds or ***fulachta fiadh*** are the commonest prehistoric site type recorded in Ireland with well over 4,500 known examples. The majority date to the Bronze Age though some historical examples have also been recorded. They are typically represented by piles of heat-fractured stones and a trough and are generally found close to water or in marshy ground. The function of these was to heat water though it is not clear what the heated water was then used for but suggestions include saunas, cooking and industrial processes.

A **gazebo** is a type of free-standing pavilion structure, similar to a summer-house, built to take advantage of a view and affording shelter, shade and rest. They are often situated a short distance from a main residence and used as a focal point and object of pleasure in a garden. They were particularly popular in the eighteenth century.

The **gunwale** is the uppermost timber around the sides of a boat.

A **halberd** is a pointed, broad, usually slightly asymmetrical, metal blade. Halberds are similar to daggers though unlike daggers they are mounted at roughly right angles to a haft and secured by rivets. They date to the Early Bronze Age.

A **henge** is form of prehistoric earthwork that was built in Ireland and Britain during the Late Neolithic and Early Bronze Age. They are circular in form, delimited by an internal ditch and external bank. Given this arrangement they are therefore considered to have served a ritual rather than a defensive purpose. Henges can enclose stone circles, timber circles, burials and other features.

A **hill fort** is a type of defensive earthwork located on elevated ground constructed and used during the Late Bronze Age and Iron Age. The fortifications usually follow the contours of the hill and consist of one or more ramparts made of earth, stone and/or wood, with an external ditch.

Inhumation burials are interments of the dead, unburnt, in the ground. The term is used to differentiate unburnt from burnt burials (cremations).

The **La Tène** culture was a European Iron Age culture (fifth to first century BC). It was named after the archaeological site of La Tène, near Lake Neuchâtel in Switzerland, where a large collection of artefacts was discovered at the end of the nineteenth century. The La Tène art style is characterised by inscribed spirals, interlaces and stylised curvilinear animal and vegetal forms typically executed on bronze vessels, armour and horse accessories. La Tène cultural material has been found over a large area of Central and Western Europe, including Ireland and Great Britain. Some of the societies that are archaeologically identified with La Tène material culture were identified by Greek and Roman authors as *keltoi* ('Celts') and *galli* ('Gauls').

A **lintel** is a horizontal piece of wood or stone supported by two vertical posts at either end. Lintels are typically used above an opening, such as a window or door, in a load-bearing wall to support the weight of the structure above.

Machicolations are openings in the floor of a gallery or a projecting defensive parapet of a castle or tower or other defensive structure, through which combustibles, scalding water, molten lead and stones, can be dropped upon assailants below.

Medieval Ulster coarse pottery is a type of coarse, unglazed, Medieval pottery found in Ulster which was mainly used for cooking and storage. It emerged in east Ulster in the mid-thirteenth century AD and continued in use, with some progression and evolution in form and decoration, until the seventeenth century. It is sometimes thought to be a successor to the native Irish Souterrain Ware although its form and many of its decorative motifs are also suggestive of links with the coarse potting traditions of south-west England and Medieval Leinster. Formerly known as 'Everted Rim Ware' as the majority, though not all, have everted rims.

The **Mesolithic** ('Middle Stone Age'; 7000–4000 BC) period represents the earliest recorded evidence for human settlement in Ireland and precedes the Neolithic. It dates to several millennia after the melting of the ice sheets (approximately 10,000 BC) and by which stage the temperatures had improved, the sea levels had risen and Ireland had become an island. Mesolithic inhabitants were hunter-gatherers and lived a nomadic existence following seasonal migrations of fish, mammals and birds, harvesting nuts and fruits, collecting shellfish and acquiring raw materials, in particular flint, to make stone tools (flint axes, microliths, scrapers).

Mottes were the castles of the Anglo-Norman barons and the majority were built in the later twelfth and early thirteenth centuries AD. They take the form of a large artificial circular earthen mound with a flattened top, surrounded by a ditch and surmounted by a timber tower (which don't survive), or, occasionally by a stone tower. About a quarter of Irish mottes are also attached to a bailey or defended outer court.

A **mullioned** window is one that is subdivided with vertical bars, usually of stone or wood, known as **mullions**. A horizontal dividing bar is known as a transom.

A **murder-hole** is a hole in the ceiling of a room, corridor, stairway or gateway through which defenders can fire weapons or throw rocks or other objects down upon attackers. They are common in Irish tower houses.

The **Nine Years' War** took place in Ireland from 1594 to 1603. It was fought between the forces of the Gaelic Irish chieftains, led by Hugh O'Neill, and the armies of the Elizabethan English, and was mainly fought in Ulster. It ended in defeat for the Irish chieftains, which led to their exile in the 'Flight of the Earls' in 1607 and to the Plantation of Ulster.

Ogham is an Early Medieval alphabet primarily used in the fifth and sixth centuries AD though it originated in the fourth century or earlier. The script is formed by a series of strokes and notches. The majority of the inscriptions that survive are as stone carvings and consist of personal names.

An **orthostat** is an upright stone or slab set into the ground.

The Pale was the part of Ireland that was directly under the control of the English Crown from the late twelfth century AD following the Anglo-Norman/Cambro-Norman invasion of Ireland. By the late 1400s it had contracted to an area along the east coast stretching from Dalkey in the south to Dundalk in the North, and inland for some 64 kilometres.

Palstave axes are early types of metal axes typically made of bronze. They were hafted by means of a forked or split wooden handle kept in place with flanges and sometimes a side-loop.

A **passage tomb** is a form of Neolithic megalithic tomb. They comprise a stone-lined passage leading to a main chamber, which may be a simple single chamber or subdivided with smaller chambers set off a central area. The passage and chambers are covered by a mound of earth and stones, with kerb stones set around its edge. Art work is sometimes found carved on the orthostats and kerb stones and finds from the tombs include pins, pottery, flint implements and other stone objects. Passage tombs are often clustered together as at the bend of the River Boyne in County Meath where the most famous example in Ireland, Newgrange, is located.

A **penstock** is the term given to the pipe that delivers water to turn the blades that power a watermill.

Periodontal refers to the area occurring around and supporting the teeth and includes both bone and soft tissues.

A **perron** is an outdoor platform or terrace set at the top of a single or double flight of steps and situated outside the entrance to a mansion, church or other grand building. They were popular formal garden features in the eighteenth and nineteenth centuries in Europe.

Plate glass is a type of flat glass. Hand-blown plate glass was made by a variety of processes from the late seventeenth century until the end of the nineteenth century when machine manufactured glass took over. It often involved heavy grinding and polishing of both sides of the glass surfaces and typically produced relatively small panes.

Portal tombs, or portal dolmens, are the simplest form of Neolithic megalithic tomb. These are single-chambered tombs built of orthostats supporting a capstone. Some or all would have been covered by a cairn but this only rarely survives. Excavations have produced much the same finds as from court tombs – Neolithic pottery, stone beads and flint tools, and like court tombs, their distribution is mainly, though not exclusively, in the northern half of Ireland.

The **prehistoric** period relates to the time before written records began.

Radiocarbon dating is a scientific dating method. It can be applied to most organic materials and spans dates from a few hundred years ago to about 50,000 years ago. The radiocarbon date indicates when the organism was last alive (not when the material was used). The radiocarbon formed in the upper atmosphere is mostly in the form of carbon dioxide and is taken up by plants through photosynthesis. All animals in the food chain get their carbon indirectly from plant material, even if it is by eating animals which themselves eat plants. The net effect is that all living organisms have the same radiocarbon to stable carbon ratio as the atmosphere. Once an organism dies the carbon is no longer replaced and because the radiocarbon is radioactive, it will slowly decay away and will reduce according to the exponential decay law. Thus, by measuring the proportion of radiocarbon to stable carbon in an archaeological sample, a sheep bone for example, the amount of time that has passed since the death of that organism can be calculated. However, a radiocarbon date is not a true calendar age so the measurement needs to be calibrated using a calibration curve created by the radiocarbon dates of material of known age. (For further information see the University of Oxford's radiocarbon web-info page; **http://c14.arch.ox.ac.uk**). Radiocarbon date ranges where quoted in this book are all in calibrated (2-sigma) calendar years and are presented as calculated by the authors. Full information on the dates is published elsewhere with details of these publications given at the end of the articles.

Raths, or ringforts (also sometimes referred to as Danish forts and fairy forts), are circular or sub-circular enclosures and in their simplest form comprise a single bank and external ditch (univallate raths) enclosing a farmstead. They were constructed in a variety of forms including those with multiple banks and/or ditches (multivallate raths), elevated 'raised raths' and those built with drystone walls (cashels). Documentary sources indicate that these were occupied by the more affluent landholding class of society and dating evidence demonstrates that the majority were constructed and occupied from the early seventh to late ninth centuries AD. Some 45,000 raths are known from the island, though this is probably an underestimation of the original total and only a small proportion (approximately 0.5%) has been excavated.

A stone tool that has been **retouched** is one that has been modified by secondary flaking along the cutting edge.

Ring-barrow and **ring-ditch** (see barrow)

Ringfort (see rath)

A **rubbing stone** is a general term employed to describe small- to medium-sized stones with a smooth surface typically found on prehistoric sites. The stones may have been used in a number of ways perhaps as tools for the preparation of hides or textiles or for the grinding of cereal grains.

Saddle querns consist of two stones, an upper 'rubber' or 'rubbing' stone and a larger, lower 'bed stone' the shape of which resembles a saddle. The former was drawn to and fro manually across the stationary bed stone to grind grain. Saddle querns were introduced into Ireland in the Neolithic and continued in use throughout the Bronze Age.

Saintonge Ware is a type of Medieval pottery manufactured in the Saintes region of western France. The best known vessels are tall jugs with polychrome glazed decoration which are found widely across northern Europe and were probably traded alongside French wine. This pottery type has been found on Irish excavations from the later twelfth century but it is most commonly uncovered in thirteenth-century contexts.

A **scabbard** is a sheath for the blade of a sword or dagger, typically made of leather or metal.

Schmorl's nodes are indentations on the superior and/or inferior surfaces of the vertebral body that arise as a result of degeneration of the intervertebral discs.

Souterrains are underground structures that were built during the Early Medieval period, in the main from the mid eighth to mid thirteenth centuries AD. The design and layout of a souterrain can range from a short simple passage or chamber, to a complex arrangement of extensive passages and chambers. Souterrains can be earth- or rock-cut, drystone built or timber-lined, or of mixed construction.

Souterrain Ware is a type of indigenous coarse ware pottery used for storage and cooking. It dates from the seventh to the fourteenth century AD and mainly occurs in east Ulster but occasional examples have been found as far west as Fermanagh and as far south as Wicklow.

Tree-ring dating (see dendrochronology)

Vitriol or oil of vitriol is concentrated sulphuric acid. It was widely manufactured in the eighteenth and early nineteenth century for industrial applications and was used by button-makers, hatters, tanners and gilders amongst others for metal-cleaning and pickling. It was used in particular for the bleaching of linen and replaced the use of less efficient acids derived from sour milk.

A **wedge tomb** is a wedge-shaped megalithic tomb built during the Late Neolithic and Early Bronze Age. The tombs comprise a central burial chamber with a small antechamber, constructed of double-walled side walls of upright stones and roofed with lintels. The galleries are covered by cairns, often with a kerb of stones, and both the gallery and cairn usually decrease in height and width to the rear (being taller and wider at the entrance), producing a wedge shape in elevation and plan. Wedge tombs are mainly distributed in the south and west of Ireland and unlike other megalithic tombs, they are normally orientated with their entrance facing south-west rather than east.

Appendix 3

Further reading

Bartlett, T. and Jeffery, K. (eds) 1996 *A military history of Ireland*. Cambridge: Cambridge University Press.

Clinton, M. 2001 *The souterrains of Ireland*. Bray: Wordwell.

Donnelly, C.J. 1997 *Living places: archaeology, continuity and change at historic monuments in Northern Ireland*. Belfast: Institute of Irish Studies, Queen's University, Belfast.

Edwards, N. 1999 *The archaeology of early medieval Ireland*. London: Routledge.

Fry, M. 2000 *Coití: logboats from Northern Ireland* (Northern Ireland Archaeological Monographs; No. 4). Belfast: Environmental & Heritage Service, Department of the Environment.

Gillespie, R. 2007 *Early Belfast: the origins and growth of an Ulster town to 1750*. Belfast: Belfast Natural History and Philosophical Society, in association with the Ulster Historical Foundation.

Hamlin, A.E. 2008 *The archaeology of early Christianity in the North of Ireland* (BAR British Series 460). Edited by T.R. Kerr. Oxford: Archaeopress.

Hamlin, A. and Lynn, C. (eds) 1988 *Pieces of the past. Archaeological excavations by the Department of the Environment for Northern Ireland 1970–1986*. Belfast: HMSO.

Horning, A., Ó Baoill, R., Donnelly, C. and Logue, P. (eds) 2007 *The post-medieval archaeology of Ireland* (IPMAG Proceedings 1). Dublin: Wordwell.

Kerr, T.R. 2007 *Early Christian settlement in north-west Ulster* (BAR British series: 430). Oxford: Archaeopress.

MacCárthaigh, C. (ed.) 2008 *Traditional boats of Ireland : history, folklore and construction*. Cork: Collins Press.

Mallory, J.P. and McNeill, T.E. 1995 *The archaeology of Ulster. From colonization to plantation*. Belfast: Institute of Irish Studies, Queen's University, Belfast.

McErlean, T., McConkey, R. and Forsythe, W. 2002 *Strangford Lough: an archaeological survey of the maritime cultural landscape* (Northern Ireland Archaeological Monographs; No. 6). Belfast: Blackstaff Press.

Neill, K. 2009 *An archaeological survey of County Armagh*. Belfast: TSO Ireland.

Ó Baoill, R. 2008 *Carrickfergus: the story of the castle and walled town*. Belfast: TSO Ireland.

Raftery, B. 1997 *Pagan Celtic Ireland. The enigma of the Irish Iron Age*. London: Thames & Hudson.

Rynne, C. 2006 *Industrial Ireland 1750–1930: an archaeology*. Cork: Collins Press.

Stout, M. 1997 *The Irish ringfort* (Irish settlement studies; No.5). Dublin: Four Courts Press.

Waddell, J. 2008 *The prehistoric archaeology of Ireland.* Galway: Galway University Press.

Useful websites

NIEA: Built Heritage Directorate – NIEA website with information on legislation, grants, scheduled and State Care monuments, listed buildings and the MBR (including the Sites and Monuments Register, Register of Historic Parks and Gardens, Defence Heritage database and Industrial Heritage Records): **http://www.ni-environment.gov.uk/built-home.htm**

UAS – Ulster Archaeological Society: **http://uas.society.qub.ac.uk/**

YAC – Young Archaeologists Club, Queen's University, Belfast branch:
http://www.qub.ac.uk/schools/gap/NewsandEvents/Events/YoungArchaeologistsClub/

Plate A.1 An imported twelfth-century bowl, modified for hanging, recovered from the River Blackwater, above Charlemont, County Armagh (photograph reproduced courtesy of the Trustees of National Museums Northern Ireland).

Appendix 4

Information on access to sites

Information on access to the sites featured in this book is outlined below and grid references for the same are given in the table in Appendix 6. There is no public access to sites on private land unless otherwise stated. Further information on monuments in State Care can be found in the recently reissued *Guide to the Historic Monuments of Northern Ireland in State Care* published by NIEA (2009) and at the website **http://www.ni-environment.gov.uk/places_to_visit_home/historic-monuments.htm**. It should also be noted that many of the artefacts discussed in the book are on display in the Ulster Museum including the Drumadoon bell shrine, Killymoon gold ornaments and Clonmore shrine, as well as examples of glassware from Edward's glasshouses at Ballymacarett, Belfast.

Chapter 1

The sites at *Ballyharry* (County Antrim), *Ballyprior Beg* (County Antrim) and *Corrstown* (County Londonderry) are all on private land that has been redeveloped. No upstanding remains are visible.

The mound (rath and motte) at *Drumadoon* (County Antrim) and bawn at *Movanagher* (County Antrim) are both extant but on private land.

Chapter 2

The Neolithic ritual timber structure at *Ballynahatty* (County Down) is on private land and there are no visible upstanding remains. The adjacent Giant's Ring (henge and portal tomb) is in State Care and is open to the public.

The stone circles at *Copney* (County Tyrone) are in State Care but are on private land.

Navan Fort (County Armagh) is in State Care and is open to the public. The Navan Centre, run by the local council, is located adjacent to the monument and is open all year (see **htttp://www.armagh.co.uk**).

Lisburn Castle Gardens (County Antrim) are open to the public (see **www.castlegardenslisburn.com**).

Chapter 3

The *Greyabbey Bay logboat* (County Down) is scheduled and lies within the scheduled conservation area of the Greyabbey Bay foreshore, owned and managed by the National Trust. The Lough's foreshore is also a designated Ramsar wetland site. For further information contact The Strangford Lough Wildlife Centre.

The wreck of the *Taymouth Castle* (County Antrim) lies on the seabed under many metres of water. It is therefore only accessible to divers who should not interfere in any way with the site.

The *Dunnyneill Islands* (County Down) are in private ownership.

Chapter 4

The monastery at *Nendrum* (County Down) is in State Care and is open to the public.

The WWT Wetland Centre at *Castle Espie* (County Down) is open to the public (see **http://www.wwt.org.uk/visit-us/castle-espie**).

The sites at *Ballymacarett*, Belfast (County Antrim), *Killymoon* (County Tyrone) and *Annadale*, Belfast (County Antrim) are all on private land that has been redeveloped. No upstanding remains of the archaeological sites are visible.

Chapter 5

Castle Hill, Dungannon (County Tyrone) is open to the public. There is also an associated exhibition on display in Ranfurly House (open to the public), located adjacent to Castle Hill on the Market Square.

Newry and Mourne Museum is housed in *Bagenal's Castle*, Newry (County Down) and is open to the public (see **www.bagenalscastle.com**).

Bellaghy Bawn (County Londonderry) is in State Care and is open to the public.

The site of the *Battle of the Yellow Ford* (County Armagh) is on private land.

Chapter 6

Newtownstewart Castle (County Tyrone) is in State Care and is open to the public.

Ballintaggart (County Down) is on private land that has been redeveloped. No upstanding remains are visible but there are information boards about the excavation located in a picnic area just off the A1 Belfast to Newry road beside Loughbrickland Lake (just south of Loughbrickland).

The site of the church and graveyard at *Solar* (County Antrim) is on private land.

St Patrick's Church, Armoy (County Antrim) is in everyday use and the round tower is in State Care. Both are open to visitors.

Appendix 5

Acknowledgements

This book is essentially a successor to *Pieces of the Past* which is an edited volume (edited by Ann Hamlin and Chris Lynn) published in 1988 and which reviews the results from 34 excavations carried out by NIEA staff throughout Northern Ireland during the period from 1970 to 1986. This current project was initiated in 2003 by Brian Williams, Assistant Director of NIEA: Built Heritage Directorate. John O'Neill, former Excavation Director with the Centre for Archaeological Fieldwork (CAF) at Queen's University, Belfast initially took the helm before the task was passed briefly to Philip Macdonald (CAF) and then on to the current editorship in 2008.

Along with Brian, John and Philip, there are many other people we would like to thank who have assisted in bringing this book through to publication. First and foremost we are grateful to the many contributors to this volume without whom the book could not have been produced, and who also kindly replied to numerous queries during the editing process. Acknowledgements must also be extended to all of the excavation crews on the various sites, the landowners who generously allowed access to those sites, the archaeological companies who managed the projects and the various companies and institutions that funded the excavations (for full details see Appendix 6).

We also wish to thank the many individuals who have provided help and advice at various stages in bringing this book together, in particular Colm Donnelly (CAF), Ruairí Ó Baoill (CAF), Robert Heslip (Belfast City Council), Finbar McCormick (QUB), Cormac McSparron (CAF), Jenny and Vivien Murray, and Robin Sinton. Isabel Bennett, editor of the *Excavations Bulletin*, and Kim Rooney (NIEA) kindly provided the data used in the figures in the Preface. We would also like to thank the past and present members of NIEA's Development Control Team.

In addition to the authors, a number of other people helped with the sourcing of the many images used, and, from NIEA, we would like to thank Joe Breen, Lorraine Bourke, Tony Corey, Anthony Kirby, Helen Murphy, Gail Pollock and in particular Gareth Edwards. Other images were kindly provided by Ken Abraham (Newry and Mourne Museum), Kim Mawhinney and Michelle Ashmore (Ulster Museum), and Brenda Collins and Elaine Flannigan (the Irish Linen Centre and Lisburn Museum). Thanks also to Eoin Lennon who prepared the illustrations.

Lastly we would especially like to thank Brian Williams for his sustained encouragement in bringing this volume to completion and also, to Chris Lynn and Terence Reeves-Smyth, for proofreading and providing advice on earlier drafts of the text.

Appendix 6

Table detailing the archaeological companies and institutions that undertook and financed the excavations summarised in this book (listed by chapter). The county, national grid reference and year(s) of excavation are also given.

Chpt.	Site name	Co.	Grid reference	Year(s) of excavation	Excavation company/ Institution	Financed by
1	Ballyharry	ANT	J 469981	1996	ADS Ltd	Premier Power
1	Ballyprior Beg	ANT	D 445020	2000	CFA Archaeology Ltd	NIE Ltd
1	Corrstown	LDY	J 029468	2002–2003	ACS Ltd	The Kennedy Group
1	Drumadoon	ANT	D 167404	2003	CAF; NIEA	NIEA
1	Movanagher	ANT	C 920158	1999	author	NIEA
2	Ballynahatty	DOW	J 326677	1990–2000	QUB	QUB and NIEA
2	Copney	TYR	H 599780	1994	NIEA	NIEA
2	Navan Fort	ARM	H 847452	1998–1999	NIEA; QUB	NIEA
2	Lisburn Castle Gardens	ANT	J 269643	2003 and 2006	ADS Ltd	Heritage Lottery Fund and Lisburn City Council
3	Greyabbey Bay logboat	DOW	J 574669	2000	CMA; NIEA	NIEA
3	Dunnyneill Island	DOW	J 547538	2002–2003	CAF; QUB	NIEA
3	Clonmore (River Blackwater)	ARM	H 880610	1930s-2001	UM	UM
3	Shanmullagh (River Blackwater)	ARM	H 842533	1930s–2001	UM	UM
3	Taymouth Castle	ANT	D 260345	1995	CMA; NIEA	NIEA
4	Killymoon	TYR	H 827771	1995	NIEA	NIEA
4	Nendrum	DOW	J 526637	1999–2001	CMA; NIEA	NIEA
4	Ballymacarett (Belfast)	ANT	J 348745	2008–2009	Gahan & Long Ltd	The Carvill Group
4	Castle Espie	DOW	J 493673	2006–2008	NAC Ltd	Wildfowl and Wetlands Trust (WWT)
4	Annadale (Belfast)	ANT	J 343712	2003	NAC Ltd	Northwin Developments
5	Castle Hill (Dungannon)	TYR	H 799626	2007	CAF; NIEA; Channel 4's *Time Team*	NIEA and Time Team
5	Bagenal's Castle (Newry)	DOW	J 087261	1999–2000	Margaret Gowan & Co. Ltd; ADS Ltd	Newry and Mourne District Council and the Heritage Lottery Fund

Chpt.	Site name	Co.	Grid reference	Year(s) of excavation	Excavation company/ Institution	Financed by
5	Yellow Ford	ARM	H 845515	2001 and 2004	authors	authors
5	Bellaghy Bawn	LDY	H 953963	1989–1990	NIEA	NIEA
6	Newtownstewart Castle	TYR	H 402858	1999	NIEA	NIEA
6	Ballintaggart	DOW	H 100380	2004–2005	NAC Ltd	Jacobs Engineering UK Ltd on behalf of DRD Roads Service
6	Solar	ANT	D 344122	1993	NIEA	NIEA
6	St Patrick's Church, Armoy	ANT	D 009046	1997	NIEA	NIEA